DON'T JUST SIT THERE

D1543608

For Ages 3-5

Bible
Stories
That
Move
You

Also available from Abingdon Press:

Don't Just Sit There:
Bible Stories That Move You
For Ages 6-8

Editor: Daphna Flegal
Production Editor: Betsi Hoey
Designer: Paige Easter
Cover Photo: Ron Benedict
Illustrator: Robert S. Jones
Sign language illustrator: Barbara Upchurch

DON'T JUST SIT THERE

Bible Stories That Move You

Abingdon Press
Nashville

DON'T JUST SIT THERE:
BIBLE STORIES THAT MOVE YOU
FOR AGES 3-5

Copyright © 1997 Abingdon Press

ISBN 0-687-12210-4

Unless otherwise noted, Scripture quotations are from the New Revised Standard Version Bible. Copyright © 1989 by the Division of Christian Education of the National Council of the Churches of Christ in the USA. Used by permission. Scripture quotations identified as *Good News Bible* are from the *Good News Bible: The Bible in Today's English Version*. Old Testament: Copyright © American Bible Society 1976, 1992; New Testament: Copyright © American Bible Society 1966, 1971, 1976, 1992. Used by permission.

99 00 01 02 03 04 05 06 —10 9 8 7 6 5 4 3

MANUFACTURED IN THE UNITED STATES OF AMERICA

Table of Contents

Nehemiah, Josiah

Ruth, Naomi, Jonah, Esther, Daniel

Psalms, Proverbs

Christmas

Jesus Grows

Followers of Jesus

Jesus and the Children

Parables and Teachings of Jesus

Easter

Pentecost and the Early Church

Paul and Friends

Sunday School, The Bible, and Other Things

You don't have to sit still to learn Bible stories!

Young children learn with their whole bodies. They have short attention spans. They are energetic. And they just don't sit still. The stories in *Don't Just Sit There: Bible Stories That Move You* are designed with young, active children in mind. The stories are short and interactive. Movement, sensory experiences, story props, and rhythm are used to teach the Scriptures and get your children actively learning.

Our bodies are amazing! We have eyes to see, hands to touch, tongues to taste, ears to hear, noses to smell, and feet to move. All of these wonderful parts were created by God. And all of these wonderful parts can be used to help us learn the Bible.

So enjoy using these stories with your children, and remember — God put the wiggle in those amazing bodies!

Use these tips to get your stories moving:

1. Make sure your storytelling space gives the children room to move without bumping into each other.

2. Practice the story before using it with the children. Make sure you know the motions or how to handle the props.

3. Vary your voice. Create excitement by speaking louder and more quickly. Build suspense by speaking quietly and more slowly. Pause when you want to emphasize or create a sense of expectation.

4. Keep eye contact with your children. This is a surprisingly effective way to keep control of the group.

5. Show the children the Bible each time you tell a story. Remind the children that these stories are from the Bible.

Creation

God Has Planned a Beautiful World
by Daphna Flegal

God has planned a beautiful world,
(Sweep arms up over head,
then down to make a big circle.)
And created it with care.
(Place hands over heart.)
A glowing sun, a shining moon,
(Make circle over head.)
With light for all to share.
(Open up arms, with fingers spread wide.
Sweep hands down at sides.)

God has planned a beautiful world,
(Sweep arms up over head,
then down to make a big circle.)
And created it with care.
(Place hands over heart.)
The water with fish and the land with plants,
(Place palms together to make fish.
Wiggle as if swimming.)
With fruit for all to share.
(Pretend to eat an apple.)

God has planned a beautiful world,
(Sweep arms up over head,
then down to make a big circle.)
And created it with care.
(Place hands over heart.)
Animals of all shapes and sizes,
(Hold hands in front of body like paws.)
Birds that fly high in the air.
(Flap arms.)

God has planned a beautiful world,
(Sweep arms up over head,
then down to make a big circle.)
And wants us to give it care.
(Place hands over heart.)
For God created each person,
(Point to each other.)
And gave us the world for all to share.
(Hold arms out, turn around.)

Based on Genesis 1.

God's Good Creation

by Susan Isbell

In the very beginning of time, before there were any people, or animals, or night, or day, there was God. The world was dark *(Cover eyes with hands.)* and covered with water. *(Ripple fingers like water.)* God decided to create a world.

God created the sky. *(Point upward for sky.)* God created the water *(Make a rippling motion.)* and the land. *(Make a patting motion for land.)* God said, "This is very good." *(Nod head yes.)*

God created plants and flowers and great trees with tall branches. *(Wave arms overhead like tree branches).*

God created the sun, *(Make a large circle overhead.)* the moon, *(Make a smaller circle.)* and the stars. *(Flick fingers.)* God said, "This is very good." *(Nod head yes.)*

God created many, many creatures. Creatures that swim *(Make fish motions.)* and creatures that fly. *(Make bird motions.)* Animals that walk, like cows, *(Pretend to walk on all fours.)* animals that creep, like snakes, *(Make a slithering motion with arms.)* and wild animals, like lions and tigers. *(Make a roaring sound.)* God said, "This is very good." *(Nod head yes.)*

God created people. People who can think *(Point to head.)* and feel *(Cross arms in front of chest to indicate love.)* and care for all of God's world. God said, "This is very good." *(Nod head yes.)*

When the world was finished, God was very pleased. God liked the earth and the sky, the day and the night, the plants, trees, fish, birds, and animals. Most of all, God liked the people who would care for the earth and everything in it. Once again, God said, "This is very good." *(Nod head yes.)*

Based on Genesis 1:1-31.

Creation Sounds

by Daphna Flegal

I am putting you in charge of the fish, the birds, and all the wild animals.
Genesis 1:28, *Good News Bible*

• **Say: God plans for people to be in charge of the fish, birds, and animals. This means we are to take care of these animals and the world in which we all live. Listen to me read our Bible verse from the Book of Genesis.**

• Read Genesis 1:28 to the children.

• **Say: I'm going to read part of this verse again, and I want you to help me by making the sounds of the fish, the birds, and the wild animals.**

• Instruct the children to make the following noises for each animal:

Fish: *popping noises with their lips, like a fish blowing bubbles.*
Birds: *tweet, tweet.*
Wild animals: *grrrrr.*

• Read, "I am putting you in charge of the *fish*, the *birds*, and all the *wild animals*." Give the children time to make the noises for each italicized word.

Based on Genesis 1:28.

God Created Day and Night
by Daphna Flegal

Emphasize the words printed in bold. Encourage the children to do the motions as suggested.

In the beginning,
God created the heavens and the earth.
The earth was **dark**.
(Cover eyes with hands.)

Then God said, "Let there be **light**!"
(Uncover eyes.)
And there was **light**.
And God saw that it was good.

God called the **dark**ness night.
(Cover eyes with hands.)
God called the **light** day.
(Uncover eyes.)

And God said,
"Let there be lights in the sky."
God made the sun to shine during the day.
God made the moon and the stars to shine during the night.

God called the **dark**ness night.
(Cover eyes with hands.)
God called the **light** day.
(Uncover eyes.)
And God saw that it was good.

Based on Genesis 1:1-5, 14-19.
© 1996 Cokesbury.

Day and Night
by Bettye Saunders

God planned the sun to make the day.
(Show finger puppet with sun on it.)
And we go out to work and play.
Then when the sun goes out of sight,
(Put sun behind back.)
God planned the moon to make the night.
(Show finger puppet with moon on it.)

Based on Genesis 1:1-5, 14-19.
© 1996 Cokesbury.

Make Sun and Moon Finger Puppets
Supplies: crayons, scissors, tape

Directions
• Copy the sun and moon finger puppets for each child. Let the children color the finger puppets with crayons. Cut out the finger puppets for younger children. Older children may cut out the finger puppets themselves using safety scissors. Help each child fold the finger puppets on the dotted line. Tape the sides of the puppets together.

• Help each child put the puppet of the sun on a finger of one hand, and the puppet of the moon on a finger of the other hand.

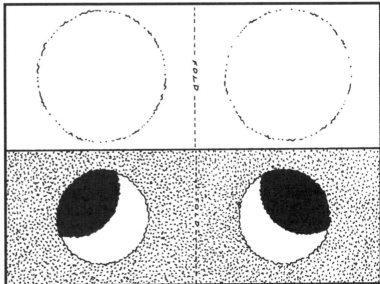

God Made Things That Fly

Say the story with a rap-like rhythm.

God made the world and the
things that fly.
God made the birds and the butterflies.
Flap, flap.
(Move arms like wings.)
Clap, clap, clap.
(Clap hands.)
Flap, flap.
(Move arms like wings.)

God made the fireflies lighting up the sky.
God made the eagles flying up so high.
Flap, flap.
(Move arms like wings.)
Clap, clap, clap.
(Clap hands.)
Flap, flap.
(Move arms like wings.)

God made the bumblebees
buzzing all around.
God made the ladybugs flitting to the
ground.
Flap, flap.
(Move arms like wings.)
Clap, clap, clap.
(Clap hands.)
Flap, flap.
(Move arms like wings.)

Based on Genesis 1:20-23.
© 1996 Cokesbury.

Caterpillar, Caterpillar
by Daphna Flegal

Caterpillar, caterpillar, crawling
on the ground.
(Wiggle fingers with cotton balls.)
Caterpillar, caterpillar, crawling
up and down.
(Wiggle fingers.)
Caterpillar, caterpillar, curling in a ball.
*(Curl fingers into fists, hiding cotton balls.
Keep fists palms up to hide butterflies.)*
Caterpillar, caterpillar, quiet and small.
(Whisper words, hold fists still.)
Butterfly, butterfly, reaching for the sky.
(Turn fists so butterflies show.)
Butterfly, butterfly, you are
God's—and so am I!
*(Turn wrists back and forth to make
butterfly "fly.")*

Make Caterpillar to Butterfly Puppets
*Supplies: construction paper, scissors, glue, tape,
colored cotton balls, colored circle stickers*

Directions
• Use the pattern printed at right as a guide
to cut a butterfly shape out of construction
paper. Older children may cut out the butterfly shapes themselves using safety scissors.
Give each child a butterfly. Encourage the
children to decorate the butterflies by adding
colored circle stickers or by gluing small
pieces of construction paper on the wings.

• Say: Let's make caterpillar and butterfly puppets using our fingers and hands. First, let's tape cotton balls onto each of our fingers. The cotton balls will make caterpillars. When we wiggle our fingers, we can make the caterpillars wiggle.

• Provide five cotton balls per child. If possible, buy colored cotton balls. Have the children choose which hand they want to use. Ask each child to turn his or her palm face up as you put a small loop of tape on each finger of the chosen hand. Place a cotton ball on each loop of tape. Have the children wiggle their fingers.

• Say: God plans for caterpillars to grow and change. Caterpillars change into butterflies.

• Use a loop of tape to tape a butterfly onto the back of each child's hand.

• Have the children play with their puppets while you say the poem.

Based on Genesis 1:20-25.
© 1992 Graded Press.

It Is Good
by Daphna Flegal

Bright blue skies and fluffy clouds,
Soft green grass and pink seashells,
I like what I see in God's world.
What do you like to see?
(Repeat things the children name.)
It is good. It is good.
(Sign words.)

Singing birds and chirping bugs,
Quacking ducks and laughing friends,
I like what I hear in God's world.
What do you like to hear?
(Repeat things the children name.)
It is good. It is good.
(Repeat sign.)

Purple grapes and yellow squash,
Apple juice and small green peas,
I like what I taste in God's world.
What do you like to taste?
(Repeat things the children name.)
It is good. It is good.
(Repeat sign.)

Cold snowflakes and kittens' fur,
Squishy mud and Grandma's hug,
I like what I touch in God's world.
What do you like to touch?
(Repeat things the children name.)
It is good. It is good.
(Repeat sign.)

Popping corn and one red rose,
Tall pine trees and fresh damp earth,
I like what I smell in God's world.
What do you like to smell?
(Repeat things the children name.)
It is good. It is good.
(Repeat sign.)

Based on Genesis 1:31.
© 1996 Cokesbury.

It is Good.
It is Good

by Daphna Flegal

God created the sky above us.
Blue skies, gray skies, even pink skies.
God created the sky above us.
Sky above us.
(Reach arms above head.)
It is good. It is good.
(Sign words.)

God created the earth below us.
Brown earth, black earth, even red earth.
God created the earth below us.
Sky above us.
(Reach arms above head.)
Earth below us.
(Touch the floor.)
It is good. It is good.
(Repeat sign.)

God created the water around us.
Clear water, blue water, even green water.
God created the water around us.
Sky above us.
(Reach arms above head.)
Earth below us.
(Touch the floor.)
Water around us.
(Pretend to swim.)
It is good. It is good.
(Repeat sign.)

Based on Genesis 1:6-10.

The Wonder Walk

by Daphna Flegal

We're going on a wonder walk.
(Slap hands against legs like walking;
keep rhythm steady throughout story.)
I wonder what we'll see?
Here's some grass.
Can't go over it.
(Shake head no.)
Can't go under it.
(Shake head no.)
Can't go around it.
(Shake head no.)
Have to go through it.
(Rub palms together.)
Thank you, God, for grass.

We're going on a wonder walk.
(Slap hands against legs like walking.)
I wonder what we'll see?
Here's a river.
Can't go over it.
(Shake head no.)
Can't go under it.
(Shake head no.)
Can't go around it.
(Shake head no.)
Have to swim through it.
(Move arms like swimming.)
Thank you, God, for rivers.

We're going on a wonder walk.
(Slap hands against legs like walking.)
I wonder what we'll see?
Here's a tree.
Can't go over it.
(Shake head no.)
Can't go under it.
(Shake head no.)
Can't go around it.
(Shake head no.)
Have to climb up it.
(Move arms like climbing.)
Thank you, God, for trees.

Take a look around.
(Put hand above eyes and turn head.)
I wonder what we'll see?
Here's a bird.
Watch it fly.
(Flap arms like flying.)
Thank you, God, for birds.

Climb down the tree.
(Move arms like climbing.)
We're going on a wonder walk.
(Slap hands against legs like walking.)
I wonder what we'll see?
Here's a cave.
Can't go over it.
(Shake head no.)
Can't go under it.
(Shake head no.)
Can't go around it.
(Shake head no.)
Have to go inside it.
(Slap hands against legs like walking.)
Thank you, God, for caves.

Here's two big eyes.
(Point to eyes.)
Here's something soft.
(Reach as if touching.)
I wonder what it is?

It's a bear!
(Throw hands up.)
Run!
(Slap hands against legs quickly.)
Climb up the tree.
(Move arms like climbing.)
Watch the bird fly.
(Flap arms like flying.)
Climb down the tree.
(Move arms like climbing.)
Swim across the river.
(Move arms like swimming.)
Go through the grass.
(Rub palms together.)
Whew!
(Wipe hand across brow.)
Thank you, God, for bears!
(Fold hands in prayer.)

17

Noah

The Very Big Boat
by Daphna Flegal

Have the children repeat the sounds printed in italics after you each time they appear in the story.

Noah," said God. "I want you to build a very big boat."

Noah obeyed God.

Zzz-zzz. Zzz-zzz. Noah cut the wood to build the very big boat.

Bam bam. Bam bam. Noah hammered the wood to build the very big boat.

"*Zzz-zzz. Zzz-zzz,*" went the saw.

"*Bam bam. Bam bam,*" went the hammer.

Finally the very big boat was finished.

"Noah," said God. "I want you to bring two of every animal into the boat."

Noah obeyed God.

Baa-baa. Noah brought two sheep into the very big boat.

Moo-moo. Noah brought two cows into the very big boat.

Roar-roar. Noah brought two lions into the very big boat.

Squeak, squeak. Noah brought two mice into the very big boat.

Quack-quack. Noah brought two ducks into the very big boat.

Neigh-neigh. Noah brought two horses into the very big boat.

Coo, coo. Noah brought two doves into the very big boat.

Baa. Roar. Quack. The very big boat was full of animals.

Spitter spatter. It started to rain.

Spitter spatter. It rained and rained.

Spitter spatter. It rained for forty days and forty nights.

Moo. Squeak. Neigh. Noah, his family, and all the animals were safe and dry inside the very big boat.

Shh-shh. The rain stopped.

Coo-coo. Noah sent a dove out of the very big boat. The dove did not return. Noah knew that it was safe to leave the boat.

Baa. Roar. Squeak. All the animals left the very big boat.

Oooh-oooh. Noah and his family looked up into the sky. They saw streaks of red, orange, yellow, green, blue, and purple colors stretched across the sky. It was a rainbow.

"I promise that I will always care for you," said God. "I have placed my bow across the clouds to help you remember my promise."

Oooh-oooh. Noah and his family looked at the rainbow. Noah knew he could trust God's promises.

Based on Genesis 6:14, 17-22; 8:22; 9:13.

God Made a Promise

by Bettye Saunders

God told Noah to build a big boat,
(Pound the fist of one hand into the palm of the
other hand like a hammer.)
God called the boat an ark.
Noah worked and worked
and worked and worked.
He made it from trees and bark.

The animals came two by two.
(Hold up two fingers.
Bounce hand up and down.)
Do you ever wonder why?
Noah led the animals into the ark.
The ark kept them safe and dry.

It rained and rained and rained and rained.
(Hold arms up and wiggle fingers
while bringing arms down.)
But Noah trusted in God's care.
(Hug self and rock back and forth.)
He knew they were safe inside the ark,
Every rabbit and dove and bear.
Then one day the raindrops stopped.
The sky turned blue and clear.
The sun began to shine again.
(Hold arms in a circle above head to make sun.)
Noah hoped that land was near.

Finally the earth was dry.
The doors of the ark opened wide.
(Open arms wide.)
Noah led everyone out of the ark.
They were happy to be outside.

Then a rainbow appeared in the sky,
(Sweep one arm above head to make a rainbow.)
With bright colors for all to see.
It was a sign of God's promise to care,
A promise for you and me.

Based on Genesis 6:14, 17-22; 8:22; 9:13.

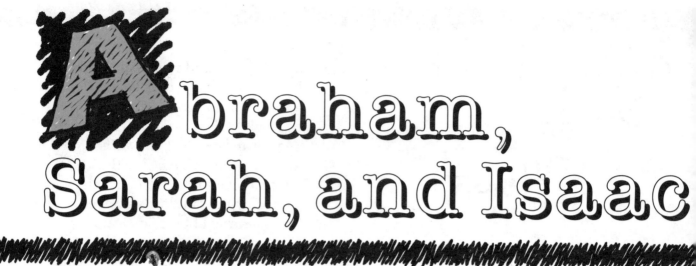

Abraham, Sarah, and Isaac

Abraham and Sarah Move

by Susan Isbell

Tell this story letting the children provide motions and sound effects for the following words:

Abraham: *stroke beard.*
Sarah: *pat cheeks.*
Donkey: *heehaw.*
Sheep and goats: *baa.*
Walking: *slap hands on legs.*

God said to **Abraham**, "Take your family, leave your home, and move to the land I will show you."

Abraham and his wife, **Sarah**, worked very hard to prepare for the long journey. **Abraham** and **Sarah** loaded everything they owned onto their **donkey**. They took down their tents. They gathered the **sheep and goats**. Soon they began **walking** to their new home.

Abraham and **Sarah**, the **sheep and goats**, and the **donkey walked** many days. Each night they would set up their tents, unload the **donkey**, and make sure the **sheep and goats** had food and water.

It was a long trip to their new home. Sometimes **Abraham** and **Sarah** would get very tired. "God is with us," **Abraham** and **Sarah** told each other. "God will take care of us and bless us."

Finally, after many days of **walking**, **Abraham** and **Sarah** let the **sheep and goats** graze in the field as they rested under a tree. As they rested, God spoke to **Abraham**.

"This is the land where you will live," God said.

Abraham and **Sarah** stopped under a big tree. They worshiped God under the tree. **Abraham** and **Sarah** thanked God for taking care of them.

Then **Abraham** and **Sarah** began to unload the **donkey**. They set up their tents. Moving had been hard for **Abraham**, **Sarah**, the **sheep and goats**, and the **donkey**, but God was with them.

Based on Genesis 12:1-9.

A New Baby

God told Abraham
Just wait and see.
(Shake finger.)
There will be a new baby
In your family.
(Pretend to rock baby in arms.)

Here's Abraham and Sarah,
(Raise index finger; also raise middle finger.)
Now wait and see.
Here's baby Isaac
(Add thumb up.)
And that's one, two, three.
(Use left index finger to touch the three raised fingers.)

Based on Genesis 17:19; 21:1-8.
© 1990 Graded Press.

The Story of Isaac

by Sue Downing

Abraham and Sarah were growing old.
(Bend over and walk.)
But, oh, how they prayed
(Fold hands in prayer.)
For a baby to hold.
(Pretend to rock baby.)
God said to each of them, "It shall be done,"
(Cross hands over heart.)
And soon they were blessed
with a beautiful son.
(Pretend to rock baby.)
They named him Isaac,
and he brought them much joy.
(Have children smile.)
He grew and grew to be a big strong boy.
(Crouch down and gradually stand up.)
Abraham then said, "A feast there will be!
(Bring hand up to mouth, as if eating.)
To thank God for Isaac and our family."
(Children will grasp each other's hands.)

Based on Genesis 17:19; 21:1-8.
© 1993 Graded Press.

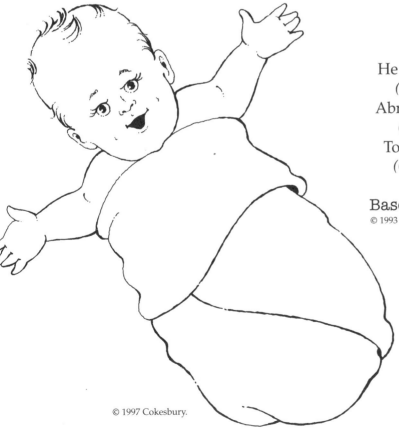

© 1997 Cokesbury.

Moses

Sister Miriam Watched

by Daphna Flegal

Rock, rock, rock. (*Pretend to rock baby.*) Mother rocked baby Moses gently in her arms. Then Mother put baby Moses into a basket.

Sister Miriam watched. (*Hold hands above eyes.*) She loved baby Moses.

Splash, splash, splash. (*Make rippling motions with fingers.*) Mother carefully placed the basket at the edge of the river.

Sister Miriam watched. (*Hold hands above eyes.*) She knew Mother was hiding baby Moses in the basket to keep him safe from Pharaoh.

Splash, splash, splash. (*Make rippling motions with fingers.*) The basket floated on the water.

Sister Miriam watched. (*Hold hands above eyes.*) She wanted to help keep baby Moses safe. Miriam hid behind the tall grasses at the edge of the river where she could see baby Moses.

Splash, splash, splash. (*Make rippling motions with fingers.*) Soon Pharaoh's daughter waded into the river to take a bath.

Sister Miriam watched. (*Hold hands above eyes.*) She knew the pharaoh's daughter was a princess.

Splash, splash, splash. (*Make rippling motions with fingers.*) The princess saw the basket floating on the river.

Sister Miriam watched. (*Hold hands above eyes.*) She saw the princess open the basket and find baby Moses.

Splash, splash, splash. (*Make rippling motions with fingers.*) Miriam waded in the water to the princess.

"Do you want me to find a woman to feed and help care for the baby?" Miriam asked the princess.

"Yes," said the princess. "Go and find someone."

Splash, splash, splash. (*Make rippling motions with fingers.*) Miriam waded out of the water. She ran to get Moses' own mother, and brought her to the princess.

Rock, rock, rock. (*Pretend to rock baby.*) Mother rocked baby Moses gently in her arms once again. Moses' mother and Miriam loved and cared for Moses as he grew.

Based on Exodus 2:1-10.

Little Baby Moses

by Elizabeth Crocker

Here is baby Moses,
(Rock arms in cradling motion.)
On the river he will float.
*(Make gentle wave motion with hand,
as if on water.)*
For Moses' mother made him
(Rock arms in cradling motion.)
A little basket boat.
(Cup hands to make a "boat.")

Sister Miriam watched,
(Place hand above eyes as if searching.)
Until the princess found him there,
(Look both ways.)
Then little baby Moses
(Rock arms in cradling motion.)
Went back to his mother's care.
(Continue rocking.)

Baby Moses grew,
(Raise hand as if indicating height.)
And became a little boy.
(Stop hand at waist level.)
Moses' mother knew
(Place index finger to temple.)
He would be her pride and joy!
*(Trace a big smile across your mouth
with index finger.)*
The princess adopted Moses,
(Hold hand at waist level.)
Just like she promised to.
(Hold hands over heart.)
The princess cared for Moses,
(Wrap arms around self as in a hug.)
While he grew and grew and grew!
(Raise hands above head.)

Based on Exodus 2:1-10.
© 1996 Cokesbury.

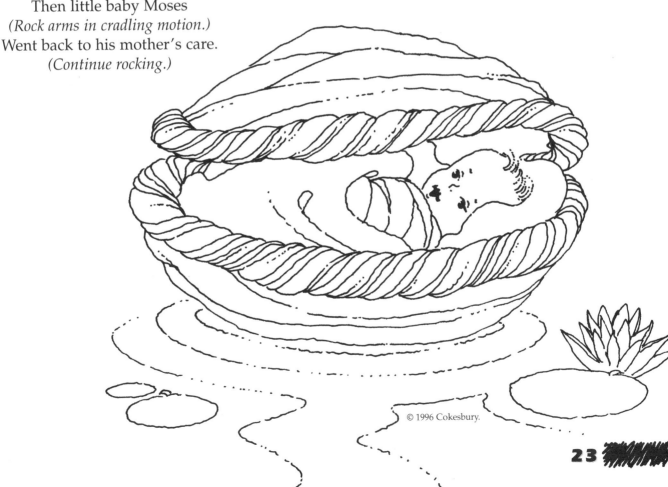

23

Let My People Go!
by Elizabeth Crocker

Moses and Aaron,
To Pharaoh they did go.
(Walk in place.)
Moses told Pharaoh:
"Let my people go!"
(Shake index finger.)

Pharaoh didn't like it.
He said, "No, no, no!
(Shake head no.)
I do not know your God,
And I will not let them go!"
(Put hands on hips.)

But God was with Moses,
God saw what Pharaoh did.
(Cross hands over heart.)
God heard God's people,
And in freedom they would live.
(Hold out arms, turn around.)

Based on Exodus 7:1-7.
© 1996 Cokesbury.

The Red Sea
by Elizabeth Crocker

Have the children help you tell the story by making sounds after certain words. Practice the following sounds:

People: *make a pattering sound by patting hands on your lap.*
Cows: *moo.*
Sheep: *baa.*
Goats: *maa.*
Sea: *make a swishing sound.*
Afraid: *"Oh no!"*
Big wind: *make a blowing sound.*

Tell the story "The Red Sea," pausing after the italicized words. Encourage the children to make the sounds.

"Hurry, hurry!" said Caleb's mother. "We must go quickly. It is time for our people to leave Egypt. Moses will lead us. Quick, bring the bread dough!" Caleb grabbed the big bowl full of dough. It had not even had time to rise.

Caleb and his family joined the others. There were more *people, cows, sheep,* and *goats* than Caleb had ever seen before. As far as he could see, there were *people* leaving Pharaoh's land and going into the desert.

Moses led the *people* toward the Red *Sea.* When the *people* reached the *sea,* the *people* saw Pharaoh and his soldiers chasing after them. The *people* were *afraid.* Caleb was *afraid* too. "Do not be *afraid,*" said Moses. "God will save us."

God told Moses to raise his walking stick over the *sea.* Caleb could hardly believe what happened next. There was a *big wind,* and God made the *sea* part. God's *people* walked through the middle of the *sea* on dry land! God's *people* were safe on the other side. The *people* were glad they had trusted God.

Based on Exodus 12:37-39; 14:5-29.
© 1996 Cokesbury.

24

The Ten Commandments

by Elizabeth Crocker

Ta-ta-ta!" came the sound of a trumpet. (*Pretend to blow a trumpet.*) The sound came from the mountain.

Swoosh, swoosh. (*Move arms in a figure eight pattern.*) The smoke was dark and thick all around the mountain.

Shake, shake. (*Shake hands.*) The whole mountain shook.

Step, step. (*Pat hands on legs.*) Moses climbed to the top of the mountain.

The mountain was a special place. (*Put tips of fingers together in a v-shape to make a mountain.*) Moses went to the mountain to talk to God. There God gave Moses rules to help the people live the way that God wanted them to live.

Love God. (*Cross hands over heart.*) First God gave Moses four rules for loving God.

There is only one God.
(*Hold up one finger.*)
Do not make other gods to worship.
(*Hold up two fingers.*)
Say my name with love.
(*Hold up three fingers.*)
Remember that Sunday is a special day.
(*Hold up four fingers.*)

These are four rules God gave to Moses.
(*Hold up four fingers.*)
Love God. (*Cross hands over heart.*)
Love others. (*Move arms out, palms up.*)
Next God gave Moses six rules for how to live together as God's people.

Love your mother and father.
(*Hold up five fingers.*)
Do not kill.
(*Hold up six fingers.*)
Show love to whoever you marry.
(*Hold up seven fingers.*)
Do not take what belongs to someone else.
(*Hold up eight fingers.*)
Do not tell lies about other people.
(*Hold up nine fingers.*)
Do not want what someone else has.
(*Hold up ten fingers.*)

These are six more rules God gave to Moses. (*Hold up six fingers.*)
Love others. (*Move arms out, palms up.*)
Step, step. (*Pat hands on legs.*) Moses climbed down the mountain.

Moses taught the people God's rules.
Love God. (*Cross hands over heart.*)
Love others. (*Move arms out, palms up.*)
They are the Ten Commandments. (*Hold up ten fingers.*)

Based on Exodus 20:1-17.

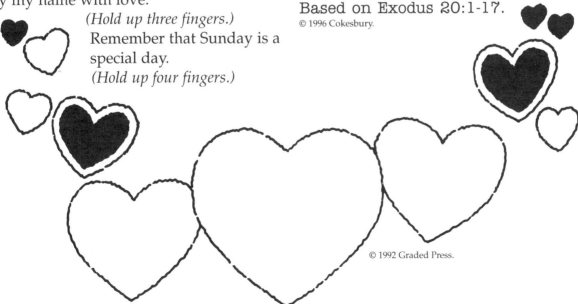

Serve God
by Elizabeth Crocker

Have the children repeat the words in italics.

Chatter, chatter, buzz, buzz! All the people were gathered together. *Chatter, chatter, buzz, buzz!* All God's people were there!

"Why are we here?" asked Michael.

"Joshua, our leader, has called us together," said his father.

"Why?" asked Michael.

"I do not know, but if we listen, Joshua will tell us," said Father.

Chatter, chatter, buzz, buzz! Michael and his father could barely hear above the noise of the crowd. *Chatter, chatter, buzz, buzz!*

Then Joshua began to speak. *Sh-h-h! Sh-h-h!* The crowd was quiet.

"You are God's people," said Joshua. "You must choose who you will serve. Will you serve the Lord your God, or will you serve someone else? As for my family and me, we will serve the Lord."

Sh-h-h! Sh-h-h! The crowd was very quiet. Then Michael's father spoke.

"Joshua," he said, "we will serve God, and we will obey God's laws." Soon others began to nod their heads. They would serve God too, they said.

Chatter, chatter, buzz, buzz! The people began to serve God together.

Based on Joshua 24:14-15, 24.
© 1996 Cokesbury.

Clap and Stomp Litany
by Elizabeth Crocker

Have the children stomp their feet as you say the verses. Have the children clap twice each time you say the refrain, **"Serve God!"** and **"Love God!"** Encourage the children to shout the refrain as they clap.

Joshua made a promise to
  (Stomp feet.)
  Serve God!
  (Clap, clap.)
Joshua and his family would
  Serve God!
Joshua asked the people to
  Serve God!
And the people said they would
  Serve God!
God taught the people to
  Love God!
With all their heart God's people should
  Love God!
With all your soul and all your might,
  Love God!
And teach your children to
  Love God!

Based on Joshua 24:14-15, 24.
© 1996 Cokesbury.

Hannah, Samuel

Hannah's Prayer

by Daphna Flegal

Hannah wanted a baby son,
(Rock a baby in your arms.)
So she went to the temple to pray:
(Fold hands in prayer.)
"If I have a son, O God,
(Rock baby.)
He'll serve you all his days."
(Cross arms over chest.)

Based on 1 Samuel 1:9-11.
© 1995 Cokesbury.

Samuel Grew

by Daphna Flegal

The Bible tells us Samuel grew
(Put hands together like an open book.)
From a baby
(Rock baby.)
To a boy.
(Hold hand up to mark height of a child.)
He helped Eli as he grew,
(Hold hands out, palms up.)
And served the Lord with joy!
(Fold hands in prayer.)
I am growing as Samuel grew
(Point to self.)
From a baby
(Rock baby.)

To a girl or boy.
(Hold hand up to mark height of a child.)
I help others as I grow
(Hold hands out, palms up.)
And serve the Lord with joy!
(Fold hands in prayer.)

Based on 1 Samuel 2:19-21.
© 1990 Graded Press.

Samuel! Samuel!

by Daphna Flegal

"I'm sleepy," said Samuel.
(Rub eyes.)
It's time for bed.
(Stretch arms above head and yawn.)
I'm going to sleep.
(Lay down on mat, fold hands under head.)
Samuel! Samuel!
(Sit up, cup hands around mouth.)
What do I hear?
(Cup hand around ear.)
Eli is calling me.
(Point to self.)
No, it's not Eli.
(Shake head "no.")
Go back to sleep.
(Lay down on mat or fold hands under head.)
Samuel! Samuel!
(Sit up, cup hands around mouth.)
Speak, Lord, I am listening!
(Cross hands over heart.)

Based on 1 Samuel 3:2-10.
© 1995 Cokesbury.

David, Solomon

David Sings Praise
by Daphna Flegal

Baa! Baa!" The sheep were happy as they ate the green grass.

"*Baa! Baa!*" The sheep were happy as they rested beside the cooling stream.

"*Baa! Baa!*" The sheep were happy as they heard the peaceful music of David's harp.

"The Lord is my shepherd," sang David. He was watching over the sheep as he sang.

God cares for me just as I care for my sheep, thought David. *God will always care for me.*

"Your house will be my house as long as I live," David continued to sing.

"I will always love you, God," David promised. "I will always try to do what you want me to do."

David was happy as he watched his sheep and sang praise to God.

"*Baa! Baa!*" said the sheep.

Based on Psalm 23.
© 1990 Graded Press.

Make Sheep Puppets
Supplies: glue, cotton balls, tape

Directions

• Make sheep puppets to use with the story.

• Copy the sheep puppet for each child. Give each child a puppet. Write the child's name on the bottom edge of the sheep.

• Let the children glue cotton balls all over their sheep puppets.

• Help each child fold the puppet along the dotted line. Glue or tape the sides of the puppet together, leaving the bottom open.

• Show each child how to slip a hand into the bottom opening of the sheep puppets. Have each child hold a sheep puppet.

• **Say: As I tell you the story, I want you to use your sheep puppets. Hold up your puppets and say "baa" each time you hear me say "baa, baa" in the story.**

FOLD

David Counts His Sheep
by Daphna Flegal

David is a shepherd,
Counting all his sheep.
(Hold up index finger on one hand to be David.)
1-2-3-4-5.
(Hold up all five fingers on the other hand to be the sheep; touch each finger with the index finger of the first hand as you count.)

David watches carefully
Until they're all asleep.
(Hold up index finger on one hand.)
1-2-3-4-5.
(Curl each finger down on the sheep hand until hand is in a fist.)

Soon the sun is rising.
"Wake up, little sheep!"
(Hold up index finger on one hand.)
1-2-3-4-5.
(Open up each finger on the sheep hand until hand is open again.)

Another day is starting.
Time to count the sheep.
(Hold up index finger on one hand.)
1-2-3-4-5.
(Touch each finger with the index finger of the first hand as you count.)

Based on 1 Samuel 16:11.

Come, Little Sheep
by Daphna Flegal

Tell the children the story "Come, Little Sheep" as if you were David. Have the children say **"baa, baa, baa"** after you say **"Come, little sheep."**

Say: Let's pretend that you are all my sheep. Each time I say "Come, little sheep," I want you to say "baa, baa, baa."

My name is David. I'm a shepherd. I take care of my family's sheep. My sheep follow me wherever I lead them. They know the sound of my voice. Come, little sheep.
Baa baa baa.
My sheep follow me to find green grass to eat. Come, little sheep.
Baa baa baa.
My sheep follow me to find cool water to drink. Come, little sheep.
Baa baa baa.
Sometimes one sheep will get lost. I look and look until I find the lost sheep. Come, little sheep.
Baa baa baa.
When it's time to sleep, my sheep follow me to a place where they will be safe for the night. It's called a sheepfold. Come, little sheep.
Baa baa baa.
While the sheep are resting, I play on my harp. My music puts the sheep to sleep. *(Whisper.)* Come, little sheep.
Baa baa baa.
(Continue to whisper.) God takes care of me just like I take care of my sheep. The Lord is my shepherd.

Based on Psalm 23.

© 1995 Cokesbury.

Samuel Finds a King
by Daphna Flegal

Samuel grew to be a man.
(Crouch down, then stand up straight.)
He served God all his days.
(Cross arms over chest.)
God wanted him to find a king
(Pretend to put a crown on your head.)
Who knew God's loving ways.
(Cross arms over chest.)
God helped Samuel find the king
(Pretend to put a crown on your head.)
From Jesse's many sons.
(Hold up several fingers.)
David had a loving heart.
(Cross arms over chest.)
God chose him to be the one.
(Pretend to put a crown on your head.)

Based on 1 Samuel 16:1-13.
© 1995 Cokesbury.

David
by Daphna Flegal

Remind the children that David played the harp.

Say: Each time I say, "God was with David," let's pretend to play the harp. Each time I say, "God is with me," point to yourself.

David was a shepherd boy.
He sang songs of praise and joy.
God was with David.
(Pretend to play the harp.)
God is with me.
(Point to self.)

When King Saul was feeling sad,
David's music made him glad.
God was with David.
(Pretend to play the harp.)
God is with me.
(Point to self.)

David and Jonathan were good friends,
On each other they could depend.
God was with David.
(Pretend to play the harp.)
God is with me.
(Point to self.)

David became king when he was a man.
He trusted God and followed God's plan.
God was with David.
(Pretend to play the harp.)
God is with me.
(Point to self.)

© 1995 Cokesbury.

Solomon Built a Temple

Have the children repeat the sounds and do the motions as you tell the story.

Wham! Wham! (*Pound fist into hand.*) Solomon heard the workers hammer the hard stone. The builders would use the large stones to make the floor of the Temple.

Crack! Crack! (*Clap hands.*) Solomon heard the workers cut the tall trees into large pieces of wood. The builders would use the wood to make the roof of the Temple.

Zzz! Zzz! (*Rub palms together.*) Solomon heard the workers saw the pieces of wood into smaller pieces. The builders would use the wood to make the walls of the Temple.

Pull! Pull! (*Pretend to pull with hands and arms.*) Solomon watched the workers drag the stones and the wood up the hill where the Temple would be built.

Work! Work! (*Pound fist into hand.*) Solomon watched the workers build the Temple for many, many years.

Hurrah! Hurrah! (*Wave hands above head.*) Finally the builders were done. Solomon and the people were happy that the Temple was finished.

Tah-rah! Tah-rah! (*Pretend to blow trumpet.*) Solomon heard the trumpets sound. All the people came to the Temple. They came to praise God.

Cre-e-ak! Cre-e-ak! (*Pretend to push open doors.*) Solomon heard the big doors of the Temple open wide.

"Come! Come!" (*Motion "come here" with hand.*) said Solomon to the people. "Let us go into the house of the Lord!"

Based on 1 Kings 5:1-12; 6:11-14; Psalm 122:1.
© 1990 Graded Press.

Solomon
by Daphna Flegal

Solomon built a house for God (*Make a fist with one hand. Use the fist to hammer the palm of the other hand.*)
To show his love
(*Put hands over heart.*)
And praise.
(*Lift both arms up.*)
When we come to church each week,
(*Walk in place.*)
We show our love
(*Place hands over heart.*)
And praise.
(*Lift both arms up.*)

Based on 1 Kings 5:1-12; 6:11-14; Psalm 122:1.
© 1990 Graded Press.

Nehemiah, Josiah

Clap Your Hands!

Have the children repeat the sounds and do the motions printed in italics. Have the children repeat the phrase, **"They thanked God and clapped their hands with joy,"** and clap their hands three times.

ong! Gong! Gong!
(Bring palms together like cymbals.)
Nehemiah and the people heard the loud crashing sounds of the cymbals. Nehemiah and the people were happy the wall around the city was finished.
They thanked God and clapped their hands with joy.
(Clap three times.)

Pling! Pling! Pling!
(Pretend to strum a harp.)
Nehemiah and the people heard the soft strumming sounds of the harps. Nehemiah and the people were happy the wall around the city was finished.
They thanked God and clapped their hands with joy.
(Clap three times.)

Tadaa! Tadaa! Tadaa!
(Pretend to blow a trumpet.)
Nehemiah and the people heard the loud blasting sounds of the trumpets. Nehemiah and the people were happy the wall around the city was finished.
They thanked God and clapped their hands with joy.
(Clap three times.)

La! La! La!
(Put hands up to mouth.)
Nehemiah and the people heard the soft singing sounds of the choir. Nehemiah and the people were happy the wall around the city was finished.
They thanked God and clapped their hands with joy.
(Clap three times.)

Tap! Tap! Tap!
(March in place.)
Nehemiah and the people heard the loud stomping sound of their feet. Nehemiah and the people marched around the wall.
They thanked God and clapped their hands with joy.
(Clap three times.)

Based on Nehemiah 12:27, 31, 38, 40, 42-43.

Josiah

When Josiah was a child
  Of eight years old,
He became king of the land,
  A very good king, we are told.

He did what was right.
He loved God with all his might.

King Josiah wore a robe.
  He wore a golden crown.
But when he sat upon the throne,
  His feet would dangle down.

He did what was right.
He loved God with all his might.

As Josiah grew and grew,
  He learned God's ways.
He was king for many years
  And loved God all his days.

He did what was right.
He loved God with all his might.

Based on 2 Kings 22:1-2.
© 1995 Cokesbury.

Make Josiah Puppets

Supplies: scissors, crayons, glue, tape, paper punch, yarn

Directions

• Make Josiah puppets to use with the story.

• Copy the Josiah puppet for each child. Cut the puppet apart along the solid lines. Give each child the puppet body, arms, and legs. Write the child's name on the back of the puppet. Let the children decorate the puppets with crayons.

• Help each child glue or tape the puppet legs and arms onto the puppet bodies. Use a paper punch to make a hole in the top of each puppet. Help each child thread a length of yarn through the hole and tie the ends of the yarn together to make a handle for the puppet.

• Show each child how to hold the handle and jiggle the puppet up and down to make the puppet move.

• Say the poem with a steady beat, emphasizing the words with the accent marks above them.

• Let the children make their Josiah puppets dance as you say the poem.

• Have the children repeat the refrain printed in bold.

• Or let the children pretend to be the Josiah puppet themselves.

• **Say: Let's pretend that you are a puppet. You have strings that move your arms and legs. Dance like a puppet.**

• Give the children a few moments to enjoy moving like puppets.

• **Say: Now let's pretend that you are a puppet of Josiah. Josiah became king when he was just a boy. Dance to the rhythm of my words as I tell you about Josiah.**

Ruth, Naomi, Jonah, Esther, Daniel

Ruth and Naomi Went to Bethlehem

Say a line and do the motion. Have the children repeat the line and the motion. Continue the poem, changing the last line to do different motions (marched, danced, jumped).

Ruth and Naomi
(Hold up index finger of one hand, then index finger of other hand.)
Went to Bethlehem.
(Sweep arm and point into distance.)
How did they get there?
(Hold hands palms up and shrug shoulders.)
They walked and walked.
(Walk in place.)

Ruth and Naomi
(Hold up index finger of one hand, then index finger of other hand.)
Went to Bethlehem.
(Sweep arm and point into distance.)
How did they get there?
(Hold hands palms up and shrug shoulders.)
They hopped and hopped.
(Hop in place.)

Based on Ruth 1:1-19
© 1997 Cokesbury.

Baby Obed

by Susan Isbell

Encourage the children to pretend to rock a baby as you say the poem in a soft voice. Or make baby Obed puppets (see at right) to use with the poem.

Sleep, baby Obed,
  Our tiny baby boy.
You have filled our home with happiness
  And brought your family joy.

Sleep, baby Obed,
  Your parents love you so,
And your grandmother, Naomi,
  Will watch you safely grow.

Sleep, baby Obed,
  Our baby boy so dear.
I'll hold you close and rock you
  Till peaceful sleep is near.

Sleep, baby Obed,
  And smile your tiny grin.
Your birth has brought great happiness
  To your family once again.

Based on Ruth 4:13-17.

Make Baby Obed Puppets

Supplies: scissors; crayons; scraps of cloth, tissue paper, or facial tissues; masking tape

Directions

• Copy the baby Obed puppet on page 38 for each child.

• Cut the puppet out along the solid lines. Give each child a puppet. Write the child's name on the back of the puppet. Let the children decorate the puppets with crayons.

• Give the children scraps of cloth, tissue paper, or facial tissues. Let the children glue the scraps onto the baby figures to make blankets for the babies.

• Cut strips of masking tape about three inches long. Tape the ends of each strip of tape onto the back of the puppets' hands. Leave a loop of space in the middle of the strip of tape.

• Show the children how to put their fingers inside the strips to manipulate the puppets' hands. Show the children how to lay their hands, puppets side up, in the crooks of their other arms and pretend to rock the babies.

• Show the children how to hold the puppet like you would a sleeping baby. Have the children rock the baby Obed puppet as you say the poem.

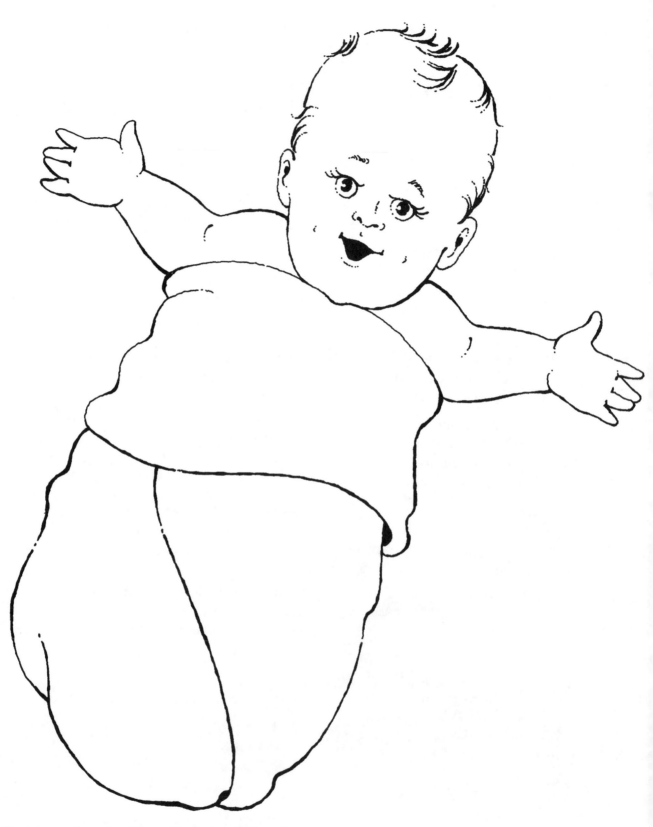

Daniel
by Daphna Flegal

Have the children fold their hands in prayer each time you say the word **Daniel**. Have the children roar each time you say the word **lions.**

"**T**hank you for this new day," **Daniel** prayed to God every morning.

"Help me make good choices," **Daniel** prayed to God every afternoon.

"Thank you for the nighttime," **Daniel** prayed to God every night.

Daniel loved God. **Daniel** worshiped God every day.

Daniel was the king's helper. **Daniel** worked very hard for the king. But there were some men who did not like **Daniel**. They wanted **Daniel's** job as king's helper. These men tried to make trouble for **Daniel**. They tricked the king into making a new rule. The new rule said that everyone had to pray to the king, not to God.

"The king is my friend," said **Daniel**. "But I cannot pray to the king. I choose to pray to God. Even though I might get in trouble, I will choose what is right."

The men watched **Daniel** pray to God. Then they ran to the king.

"**Daniel** has broken your new rule," said the men. "Now you must punish him. You must throw him to the **lions**."

The king was very sad. But the king had to obey the new rule. He put **Daniel** in with the **lions**.

"I pray that your God will take care of you, **Daniel**," said the king.

The king worried all night. He kept thinking about **Daniel** and the **lions**. The next morning the king hurried to the **lions'** den.

"**Daniel, Daniel**," cried the king. "Are you all right?"

"Yes," answered **Daniel**. "I'm fine. God closed the **lions'** mouths so they could not hurt me." **Daniel** walked out of the **lion's** den.

"I'm happy your God kept you safe," said the king. "Now I will make a new rule. Everyone will worship your God."

Daniel was glad he had made the right choice. **Daniel** continued to pray to God every day.

Based on Daniel 6:1-23, 25-28.

Lions, Lions in the Night
by Susan Isbell

Lions, lions, in the night,
Your roar can give us such a fright!
(Roar loudly.)
Daniel, Daniel, standing there,
Trust in God to hear your prayer.
(Fold hands in prayer.)
Lions, lions, in the night,
Your roar can give us such a fright!
(Roar loudly.)
Daniel, Daniel, God is near.
These lions are nothing for you to fear.
(Fold hands in prayer.)

Based on Daniel 6:1-23, 25-28.

Queen Esther
by Daphna Flegal

Esther was very beautiful. **Esther** was also kind and loving. **Esther** lived with her cousin. **Esther** and her cousin were Jews. They loved God. One day the king decided to marry a new queen. **Esther** went with her cousin to the palace to meet the king. When the king met **Esther,** he chose her to be his new queen. **Esther** was very happy. **Esther** liked being the queen and living in the palace.

Haman worked for the king. **Haman** was a selfish man. **Haman** thought he was more important than other people. **Haman** did not like the Jews. **Haman** wanted to do something to hurt the Jews. **Haman** tricked the king into making a law to kill all people who were Jews.

Queen **Esther** and her cousin were very upset. They were Jewish. "You must help our people," her cousin told Queen **Esther.** "You must talk to the king."

"I'm afraid," said Queen **Esther.** "The king might decide to kill me."

"You must be brave," said her cousin.

Queen **Esther** decided she would be brave. **Esther** asked her people to pray for her. **Esther** knew that with God's help, she could do hard things. **Esther** went to the king. **Esther** told him that she was a Jew. Queen **Esther** told the king about **Haman's** plan to kill all the Jews.

The king was very angry. He loved Queen **Esther.** He did not want the Jews killed. The king ordered his men to take **Haman** away. Queen **Esther** saved her people.

Based on the Book of Esther.

Have a Queen Esther Melodrama
Supplies: tape, crayons, scissors, craft stick

Directions:
• According to Jewish tradition, the story of Esther is told as a melodrama.

• Copy the the crown and mustache. Cut the crown pieces along the solid lines. Cut the mustache oval out of the crown front. Color the crown and tape it together. Tape the mustache onto a craft stick.

• Explain that the story is about a very brave woman named Esther. Hold up the crown picture.

• **Say: Each time I hold up the crown and say the name Esther, I want you to say "yea!"**

• Then explain that the story also has a very bad man named Haman. Hold up the mustache picture.

• **Say: Each time I say the name Haman, I want you to say "boo!"**

• Remind the children that it can be fun to boo the bad guy in a story, but that it is unkind to boo people.

• Tell the story "Queen Esther," holding up the crown and mustache at the appropriate times. Let the children enjoy saying "yea!" and "boo!"

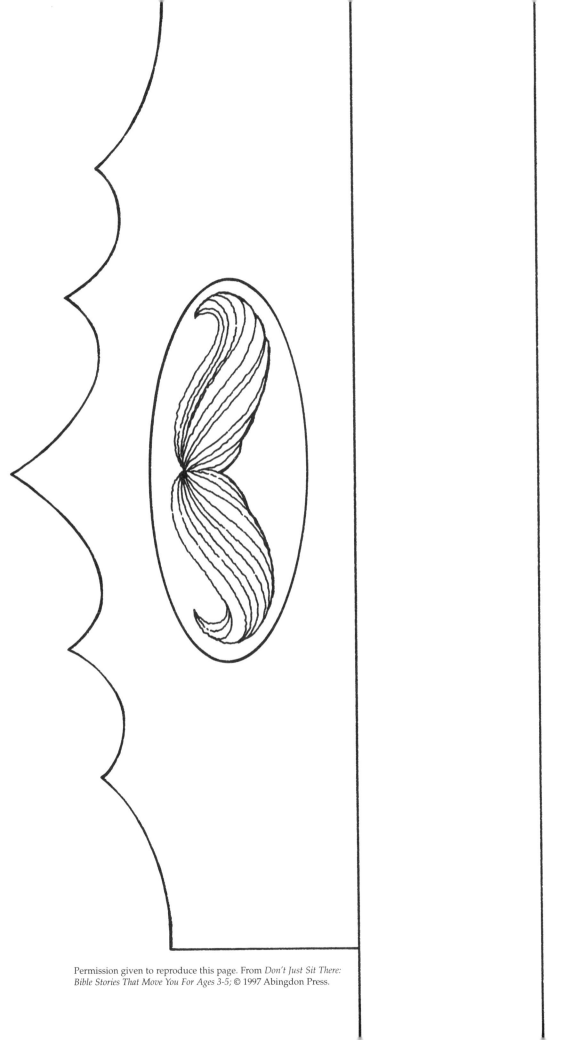

Jonah and the Big Fish
by Susan Isbell

Have the children say the repeating words and do the motions with you.

"Go, go, go, go!"
(Shake finger.)
God told Jonah one day.
"Go, go, go, go!
(Shake finger.)
To Ninevah right away!
Go, go, go, go!
(Shake finger.)
Talk to the people there.
Go, go, go, go!
(Shake finger.)
Tell them that I care."

"No, no, no, no!"
(Shake head no.)
Jonah told God that day.
"No, no, no, no!
(Shake head no.)
I'm going to run away.
No, no, no, no!"
(Shake head no.)
Jonah jumped into a boat,
"No, no, no, no!"
(Shake head no.)
Soon he was afloat.

Whoosh, whooo, splash, crash!
(Rock back and forth.)
The wind began to blow.
Whoosh, whooo, splash, crash!
(Rock back and forth.)
The boat rocked to and fro.
Whoosh, whooo, splash, crash!
(Rock back and forth.)
The sea began to rumble,
Whoosh, whooo, splash, crash!
(Rock back and forth.)
Into the water Jonah tumbled.

Gurgle, gurgle, gulp, gulp!
(Put palms together to make fish with hands.)
A fish so large and smelly,
Gurgle, gurgle, gulp, gulp!
(Put palms together to make fish with hands.)
Swallowed Jonah into its belly.
Gurgle, gurgle, gulp, gulp!
(Put palms together to make fish with hands.)
Jonah was so afraid.
Gurgle, gurgle, gulp, gulp!
(Put palms together to make fish with hands.)
"God help me!" Jonah prayed.

Hooray, hooray, hurrah, hurrah!
(Hold arms up, shake hands.)
God heard Jonah's prayer.
Hooray, hooray, hurrah, hurrah!
(Hold arms up, shake hands.)
God heard him, even there.
Hooray, hooray, hurrah, hurrah!
(Hold arms up, shake hands.)
The fish helped with God's plan.
Hooray, hooray, hurrah, hurrah!
(Hold arms up, shake hands.)
And spit Jonah upon the sand.

Based on Jonah 1:1-17; 2:1-2, 10.

Psalms, Proverbs

© 1996 Cokesbury.

Bible Songs
by Susan Isbell

Psalms is a book of Bible songs.
(Hold hands like a book.)
Listen and you will know
(Cup hand to ear.)
How Bible people gave thanks and praise
(Praying hands.)
To God so long ago.
(Arms upward.)

© 1997 Cokesbury.

God Made the Stars
by Sue Downing

God made the stars
that shine so bright,
Lighting up the sky at night.
*(Stand with feet spread wide apart
and arms outstretched to side.)*

God made the birds.
See them in the air,
Flying, flying everywhere.
*(Move arms up and down
and "fly" around the room.)*

God made the fish
that live in the sea,
Swimming all around so happily.
*(Move outstretched arms
in a backward motion.)*

God made the trees
that grow so tall,
(Stoop down and gradually stand up.)
Spreading their branches over all.
(Wave arms high above head.)

Based on Psalm 8.

© 1993 Graded Press.

God Is Good

by Susan Isbell

God is good.
(Extend both arms toward the front.)
God is great.
(Open both arms to the sides.)
Let's praise God
(Raise both arms over the head.)
And celebrate!
(Clap three times while saying "celebrate.")

The light, the dark,
The night, the day,
God created in a special way.

God is good.
(Extend both arms toward the front.)
God is great.
(Open both arms to the sides.)
Let's praise God
(Raise both arms over the head.)
And celebrate!
(Clap three times while saying "celebrate.")

The earth, the sky,
The moon, the sun,
God created everyone.

God is good.
(Extend both arms toward the front.)
God is great.
(Open both arms to the sides.)
Let's praise God
(Raise both arms over the head.)
And celebrate!
(Clap three times while saying "celebrate.")

The birds, the fish,
The plants, the trees,
God created each of these.

God is good.
(Extend both arms toward the front.)
God is great.
(Open both arms to the sides.)
Let's praise God
(Raise both arms over the head.)
And celebrate!
(Clap three times while saying "celebrate.")

Animals so big,
Animals so small,
God created one and all.

God is good.
(Extend both arms toward the front.)
God is great.
(Open both arms to the sides.)
Let's praise God
(Raise both arms over the head.)
And celebrate!
(Clap three times while saying "celebrate.")

Man and woman,
Boy and girl,
God created all the world.

God is good.
(Extend both arms toward the front.)
God is great.
(Open both arms to the sides.)
Let's praise God
(Raise both arms over the head.)
And celebrate!
(Clap three times while saying "celebrate.")

Based on Psalm 8:1-9.

Celebrate!

It's time to celebrate! Let's clap our hands and celebrate! *(Clap.)* Let's clap our hands and make happy sounds! *(Clap.)* It's time to celebrate.

Celebrate! That's a really big word. Can you say the word *celebrate*? When you have a birthday, you celebrate the day you were born. Birthdays can be a happy time. Do you like birthdays? How old are you now? Let's stop and clap for you. *(Clap.)* Let's clap for me. *(Clap.)*

We can celebrate other things besides birthdays. We can celebrate and praise God for the wonderful things God has done. We can say thank you to God. Let's think about some of the wonderful things God has done. God has made the world with birds and cats and dogs and elephants and bugs and fish and flowers and trees and rainbows. Let's thank God for the world. *(Clap.)*

God has planned for us to have bodies that walk and talk and eat and sleep and hear and see. Let's thank God for our bodies. *(Clap.)*

God has planned for people to love us and help us. Let's thank God for people. *(Clap.)* Let's thank God for you. *(Clap.)* Let's thank God for me. *(Clap.)*

Let's celebrate!

Tell of the Wonderful Things

Have the children pretend to blow trumpets each time you say, **"Praise God! Tell of the wonderful things God has done."** Or let the children make praise horns (see instructions at right).

In the beginning,
God created the heavens and the earth.
Praise God!
Tell of the wonderful things God has done.
(Hold horn up to mouth.)

God created day and night.
Praise God!
Tell of the wonderful things God has done.
(Hold horn up to mouth.)

God created sky, earth, and water.
Praise God!
Tell of the wonderful things God has done.
(Hold horn up to mouth.)

God created all kinds of plants.
Praise God!
Tell of the wonderful things God has done.
(Hold horn up to mouth.)

God created fish and water creatures.
Praise God!
Tell of the wonderful things God has done.
(Hold horn up to mouth.)

God created birds and flying creatures.
Praise God!
Tell of the wonderful things God has done.
(Hold horn up to mouth.)

God created all kinds of animals.
Praise God!
Tell of the wonderful things God has done.
(Hold horn up to mouth.)

God created people.
Praise God!
Tell of the wonderful things God has done.
(Hold horn up to mouth.)

God's creation is good.
Praise God!
Tell of the wonderful things God has done.
(Hold horn up to mouth.)

Based on Psalm 9:1.

Make Praise Horns
Supplies: crayons, scissors, tape

Directions
• Copy the praise horn for each child. Cut out the horn for younger children. Older children can cut the horn out themselves using safety scissors. Give each child a horn. Write the child's name on the horn.

• Let the children decorate the horns with crayons.

• Help each child roll the paper together to make a horn. Tape the sides of the horn together.

• Show the children how to hold the horn up to their mouths and blow.

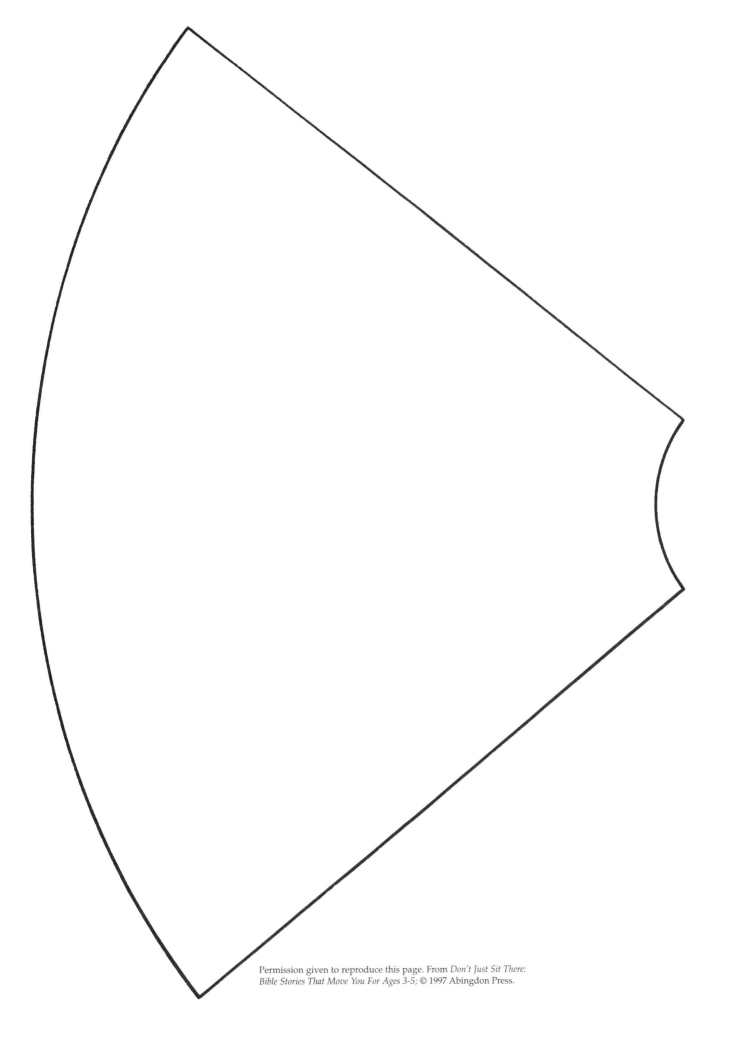

O Taste and See

by Daphna Flegal

Juicy red apples, thick chocolate cake,
Blueberry muffins ready to bake.
"O taste and see that the LORD is good!"
Sticky, sweet caramel, a sour lemon drop,
Animal crackers, corn that you pop.
"O taste and see that the LORD is good!"
Strawberry ice cream, carrots that crunch,
Yellow bananas, green grapes in a bunch,
"O taste and see that the LORD is good!"

Based on Psalm 34:8.

Directions

• Give each child a snack of one of the foods mentioned in the poem (blueberry muffins, caramel, lemon drops, animal crackers, popcorn, strawberry ice cream, carrots, bananas, green grapes). Say the poem as the children are eating.

NOTE: Be aware of any children with food allergies. Choose a food that every one can eat.

Make a Joyful Noise!

by Daphna Flegal

Clap your hands,
(Clap hands with each word.)
Stomp your feet,
(Stomp feet with each word.)
Make a joyful noise!
(Turn around.)

Pat your knees,
(Pat knees with each word.)
Tap your toes,
(Tap toes with each word.)
Make a joyful noise!
(Turn around.)

Flap your arms,
(Flap arms like bird with each word.)
Touch your nose,
(Touch nose with each word.)
Make a joyful noise!
(Turn around and sit down.)

Based on Psalm 100:1.

Worship the Lord With Joy

by Daphna Flegal

© 1995 Cokesbury.

ake happy sounds to God,
Clap, clap, clap!
(Clap hands.)
Make happy sounds to God,
Tap, tap, tap!
(Tap toes.)
Make happy sounds to God,
Snap, snap, snap!
(Tap fingers together.)
Worship the Lord with joy
And sing happy, happy songs!

**God made us,
We belong to God.**

Make happy sounds to God,
Clap, clap, clap!
(Clap hands.)
Make happy sounds to God,
Tap, tap, tap!
(Tap toes.)
Make happy sounds to God,
Snap, snap, snap!
(Tap fingers together.)
Worship the Lord with joy
And sing happy, happy songs!

**God is good,
God loves us forever.**

Make happy sounds to God,
Clap, clap, clap!
(Clap hands.)
Make happy sounds to God,
Tap, tap, tap!
(Tap toes.)
Make happy sounds to God,
Snap, snap, snap!
(Tap fingers together.)
Worship the Lord with joy
And sing happy, happy songs!

Based on Psalm 100.

© 1995 Cokesbury.

Praise God With Me

by Daphna Flegal

Praise God with trumpets.
Taadaa. Taadaa.
(Put hands to mouth like playing trumpet.)

Praise God with dance.
Tralaa. Tralaa.
(Turn around in place.)

Praise God with flutes.
Tralee. Tralee.
(Put hands to mouth like playing flute.)

Praise God with tambourines.
Tradee. Tradee.
(Shake hands like playing a tambourine.)

Praise God, praise God,
Praise God with me!
(Point to yourself.)

Based on Psalm 150.
© 1995 Cokesbury.

Praise God!

Have the children raise their arms above their heads and shake their hands each time they hear the word *praise* in the poem.

Praise God!
Praise God at church;
Praise God for all the mighty things
God has done;
Praise God because God is great!
Praise God with trumpets;
Praise God with harps!
Praise God with tambourines;
Praise God with dance;
Praise God with lutes;
Praise God with loud crashing cymbals!
Let everyone **praise** God!
Praise God!

Based on Psalm 150.
© 1995 Cokesbury.

This Is the Way!

by Sue Downing

This song is sung to the tune of "This Is the Way."

This is the way we beat the drum,
Beat the drum, beat the drum.
This is the way we beat the drum.
*(Make large drum beating
movements with hands.)*
"Make a joyful noise!"
*(Hold open hands up to mouth,
then extend hands.)*

This is the way we play the cymbals,
Play the cymbals, play the cymbals.
This is the way we play the cymbals.
*(Make big clapping motion
with outstretched arms.)*
"Make a joyful noise!"
*(Hold open hands up to mouth,
then extend hands.)*

This is the way we blow the trumpet,
Blow the trumpet, blow the trumpet.
This is the way we blow the trumpet.
*(Hold hands up as if playing a trumpet
and move fingers up and down.)*
"Make a joyful noise!"
*(Hold open hands up to mouth,
then extend hands.)*

This is the way we praise the Lord,
Praise the Lord, praise the Lord.
This is the way we praise the Lord,
(Hold arms up and wave them.)
"With a joyful noise!"
*(Hold open hands up to mouth,
then extend hands.)*

Based on Psalm 150.

Be a Friend
by Susan Isbell

Have the children shout, **"Be a friend!"** after
you say the Bible verse each time.

A friend is a person
You really enjoy.
A friend can be a girl.
A friend can be a boy.

A friend loves at all times.
(*shout*) **Be a friend!**
A friend loves at all times.
(*shout*) **Be a friend!**

A friend is a person
Who's lots of fun.
Friends can come in groups,
Or maybe just one.

A friend loves at all times.
(*shout*) **Be a friend!**
A friend loves at all times.
(*shout*) **Be a friend!**

A friend can make you laugh.
A friend can make you cry.
But a real friend gives
Love and care a try.

A friend loves at all times.
(*shout*) **Be a friend!**
A friend loves at all times.
(*shout*) **Be a friend!**

Based on Proverbs 17:17.

Christmas

Advent, Advent
by Daphna Flegal

Advent, Advent begins today.
(Cup hands around mouth.)
Let's get ready!
(Tap knees twice.)
Let's get ready!
(Shake hands above head twice.)

It's a time to sing and pray.
(Fold hands in prayer.)
Let's get ready!
(Tap knees twice.)
Let's get ready!
(Shake hands above head twice.)

Jesus' birthday will soon be here.
(Rock baby.)
Let's get ready!
(Tap knees twice.)
Let's get ready!
(Shake hands above head twice.)

Advent tells us that Christmas is near.
(Turn around.)
Let's get ready!
(Tap knees twice.)
Let's get ready!
(Shake hands above head twice.)

Get Ready!
by Susan Isbell

A prophet told the people
That one day they would see
God's promise of a special king,
And who that king would be.

Let's get ready!
(Clap hands twice.)
Let's get ready!
(Shake hands above head twice.)

A child is born to us!
He will be God's king,
A child is born to us!
And peace to all he'll bring.

Let's get ready!
(Clap hands twice.)
Let's get ready!
(Shake hands above head twice.)

So listen to the prophet,
Get ready and prepare.
Something good is coming
To people everywhere.

Let's get ready!
(Clap hands twice.)
Let's get ready!
(Shake hands above head twice.)

Based on Isaiah 9:2-7.

Good News!

by Elizabeth Crocker

Have the children do the motions and repeat the refrain.

Swish, swish, swish. *(Pretend to sweep with broom.)* Mary heard the swishing sound of the broom as she swept it across the dirt floor. *Swish, swish, swish. (Pretend to sweep with broom.)*

Suddenly a bright light filled the room. *(Cover eyes with hand.)* It was an angel! *Clunk!* Mary was so surprised, she dropped the broom. She was afraid.

"Peace to you, Mary," said the angel. *(Fold hands as if in prayer.)* "Don't be afraid. I have good news for you. You will have a baby, and you will name him Jesus! God loves you very much, Mary."

Good news, Mary! *(Cup hands around mouth.)* **You will have a baby!** *(Rock baby.)*

Joseph wondered about God's message to Mary. Zzz, zzz, zzz. *(Rest head to side on folded hands.)* One night while Joseph was sleeping, the angel brought a message to Joseph. Zzz,zzz,zzz. *(Rest head to side on folded hands.)*

"Don't be afraid, Joseph," said the angel. *(Fold hands as if in prayer.)* "I have good news. Mary will have a baby, and you are to name him Jesus. God wants you to take care of Mary and the baby. God loves you very much, Joseph."

Good news, Mary! *(Cup hands around mouth.)* **You will have a baby!** *(Rock baby.)*

Mary and Joseph loved God. *(Hold hands over heart.)* They were happy to do what the angel told them to do. Mary would have a baby, and they would name him Jesus. Good news!

Good news, Mary! *(Cup hands around mouth.)* **You will have a baby!** *(Rock baby.)*

Based on Luke 1:26-35; Matthew 1:18-24.

Great Joy

by Elizabeth Crocker

Sweep, sweep, went the broom.
(Pretend to sweep with a broom.)
The angel came to Mary's room.
(Fold hands as if in prayer.)
Peace to you! Don't be afraid!
(Shake head no.)
You know the promise God has made.
(Cross hands over heart.)
You will have a baby boy.
(Pretend to rock baby.)
He will bring the world great joy!
(Clap hands four times.)
Zzzzz, zzzz, Joseph slept.
(Rest head to side on folded hands.)
Into his dream the angel crept.
(Fold hands as if in prayer.)
Joseph, don't you be afraid.
(Shake head no.)
You know the promise God has made.
(Cross hands over heart.)
Mary will have a baby boy.
(Pretend to rock baby.)
He will bring the world great joy.
(Clap four times.)

Based on Luke 1:26-35, Matthew 1:18-24.

© 1996 Cokesbury.

Mary Rode a Donkey

by Elizabeth Crocker

Read this echo story rhythmically, as you would "Going on a Bear Hunt." Pat the tops of your legs alternately to establish a rhythm. Continue the rhythm throughout the story.

Mary rode a donkey
(Mary rode a donkey)
All the way to Bethlehem.
(All the way to Bethlehem.)

A little grey donkey,
(A little grey donkey,)
All the way to Bethlehem.
(All the way to Bethlehem.)

Joseph walked beside them
(Joseph walked beside them)
All the way to Bethlehem.
(All the way to Bethlehem.)

Down the dusty dirt road,
(Down the dusty dirt road,)
All the way to Bethlehem.
(All the way to Bethlehem.)

Gonna have a baby
(Gonna have a baby)
When they get to Bethlehem.
(When they get to Bethlehem.)

Gonna name him Jesus
(Gonna name him Jesus)
When they get to Bethlehem.
(When they get to Bethlehem.)

When will they get there?
(When will they get there?)
All the way to Bethlehem.
(All the way to Bethlehem.)

Long, long way to Bethlehem.
(Long, long way to Bethlehem.)
All the way to Bethlehem.
(All the way to Bethlehem.)

Based on Luke 2:1-5.
© 1996 Cokesbury.

Clippity Clop!
by Elizabeth Crocker

Have the children pat their legs alternately when you say **"clippity clop, clippity clop."** Or let the children make dancing donkeys (see below) to use with the story.

Clippity clop, clippity clop, went the donkey. Mary and Joseph were going to Bethlehem. *Clippity clop, clippity clop.* Mary sang a happy song as she rode on the donkey's back. *Clippity clop, clippity clop.* Joseph led the donkey. He was happy too. Soon they would have a new baby.

Clippity clop, clippity clop. It was a long way to Bethlehem. *Clippity clop, clippity clop.* Joseph and Mary traveled down the dusty dirt road. *Clippity clop, clippity clop,* all the way to Bethlehem.

"Look, Mary! We're here!" said Joseph. "I've never seen so many people. Bethlehem is a very busy place tonight!"

Clippity clop, clippity clop. Joseph led the donkey into the city. *Clippity clop, clippity clop.* Joseph could see that Mary was very tired from the long trip. *Clippity clop, clippity clop.* Joseph led Mary and the donkey to the inn.

Based on Luke 1:38, 46-47; 2:1-5.
© 1996 Cokesbury.

Make Dancing Donkeys
Supplies: scissors, crayons, glue or tape, paper clips, buttons or metal washers, paper punch, yarn

Directions
• Copy the donkey figure for each child. Cut apart the donkey along the solid lines. Give each child a donkey and a set of legs. Write the child's name on the donkey.

• Let the children decorate the donkeys with crayons.

• Help the children fold the donkey bodies along the dotted lines. Let the children make tails by gluing or taping pieces of yarn onto the donkey bodies.

• Show the children how to fold the legs back and forth like an accordion. Help the children glue or tape the legs on the bodies. Have the children glue or tape paper clips, buttons, or metal washers on the end of each leg.

Note: Always be careful when using small objects with young children.

• Use a paper punch to make holes at the top of each donkey. Help each child thread yarn through the holes. Tie the ends together. Have the children hold the donkeys by the loop and tap them on the floor or table top. The paper clips, buttons, or washers will make clicking sounds.

• Have the children tap their dancing donkeys on the table or on the floor each time you say the words *clippity clop.* Adjust your speed so that the children have time to move their dancing donkeys.

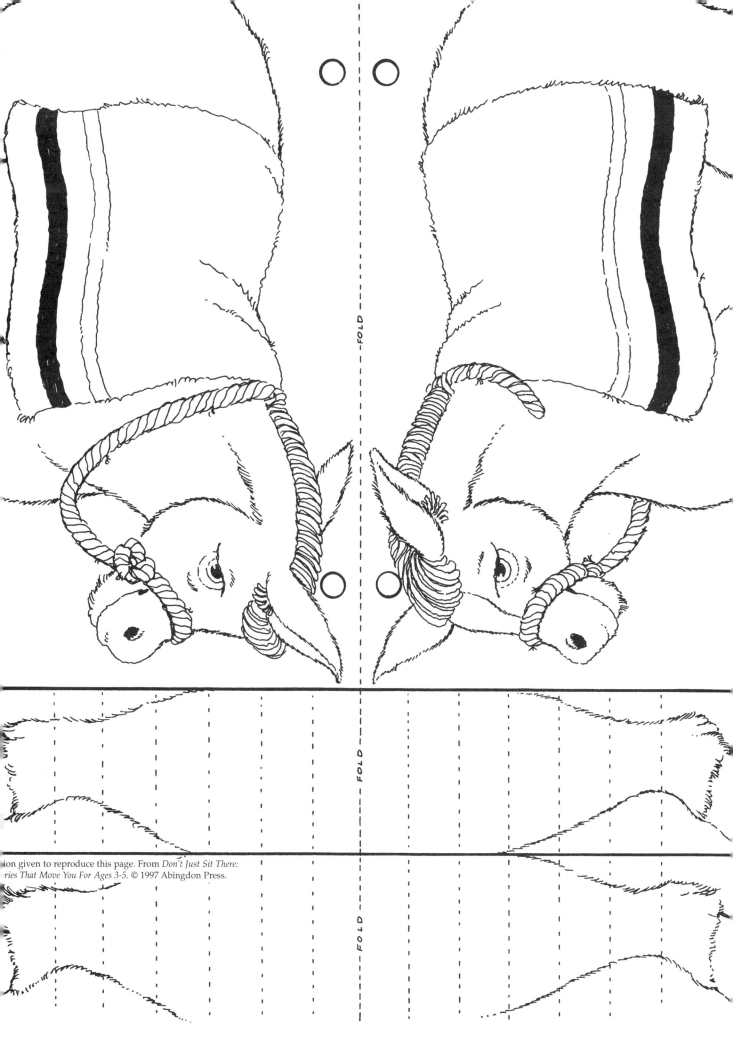

FOLD

FOLD

FOLD

© 1996 Cokesbury.

Baby Jesus Is Born
by Daphna Flegal

Have the children say the repeating words and do the motions after you.

Walk! Walk! Walk! *(Walk in place.)* Mary and Joseph walked to Bethlehem. They were tired and wanted to rest.

Knock! Knock! Knock! *(Pretend to knock on a door.)* Joseph knocked on the door of the inn.

"May we sleep here tonight?" asked Joseph.

No! No! No! *(Shake your head no.)* "I'm sorry," said the innkeeper. "I have no more room."

Turn! Turn! Turn! *(Turn around.)* Sadly, Mary and Joseph turned to walk away.

Wait! Wait! Wait! *(Hold up your hand to signal stop.)* "You may sleep in the stable," said the innkeeper. "You will be warm with the animals."

Sleep! Sleep! Sleep! *(Put your hands under your head as if sleeping.)* Mary and Joseph slept on the fresh straw.

Waa! Waa! Waa! *(Pretend to cry.)* The baby Jesus cried as Mary wrapped him in a soft blanket.

Shh! Shh! Shh! *(Pretend to rock a baby in your arms.)* Mary rocked the baby Jesus to sleep.

Sing! Sing! Sing! *(Cup your hands around your mouth.)* The angels sang the good news that Jesus was born.

Hurry! Hurry! Hurry! *(March in place.)* The shepherds hurried to find the baby Jesus.

Based on Luke 2.
© 1990 Graded Press.

A Christmas Thank-you Litany
by Sharilyn S. Adair

Use nativity figures (stable, cow, donkey, Joseph, Mary, manger, baby) to introduce each line. Encourage the children to repeat the phrase, **"Thank you, God, for baby Jesus."**

Here is the stable where Jesus was born,
Thank you, God, for baby Jesus.
A cow and a donkey to keep him warm,
Thank you, God, for baby Jesus.
Joseph and Mary to take care of him,
Thank you, God, for baby Jesus.
And a warm manger bed to lay him in.
Thank you, God, for baby Jesus.
Here is the baby, asleep in the hay,
Thank you, God, for baby Jesus.
A gift of God's love both then and today.
Thank you, God, for baby Jesus.

Based on Luke 2:7.
Copyright © 1994 Cokesbury.

© 1996 Cokesbury.

Welcome, Baby Jesus
by Susan Isbell

Tell this story using a surprise bag. In the bag have the following items:

Medium-sized rock.
Hay or straw.
Small container of oil.
Strips of cloth.

As you name each of these items in the story, take the item from the bag and pass it around for each child to see, touch, or smell.

Mary was tired. The trip to Bethlehem had been long. She and Joseph had walked and walked.

The streets were crowded. Joseph tried to find a room, but all the rooms were full. Finally someone told Joseph about a stable nearby.

Joseph helped Mary into the little stable for the animals. Mary was glad to be warm and quiet.

Mary looked at the animals in the stable. She saw the box where the animals ate their food. It was made out of *stone*. She ran her hands over the *stones* of the box. The *stones* felt strong and cool.

"This will make a nice bed for the baby," Mary said.

Joseph used *hay* to make a bed for Mary on the floor of the stable. Mary rested on the *hay*. The *hay* smelled clean and fresh.

"We will be safe and warm here for the night," Joseph said. Mary closed her eyes. She heard the gentle breathing of the cow. She heard the *"baa, baa"* of the little lamb and the cooing of the birds in the rafters above.

During the night a wonderful thing happened! Mary's baby was born.

Joseph unpacked the *cloths* Mary brought to wrap the baby in. Mary rubbed sweet-smelling *oil* on the baby's skin. She wrapped the baby in the soft *cloths*. Mary rocked the baby to sleep.

Joseph filled the animals' *stone* box with *hay* to make a soft bed for the new baby.

Joseph took the baby from Mary and laid him in the *stone* box.

"Welcome, baby Jesus," Joseph said. Mary and Joseph thanked God for their new baby.

Based on Luke 2:1-7.
© 1997 Cokesbury.

Baby Jesus

by Elizabeth Crocker

© 1996 Cokesbury.

Have the children do the motions printed in italics. Encourage the children to repeat the animal sounds after you.

Clippity clop, clippity clop. *(Pat legs alternately.)* Joseph led Mary and the donkey to the inn.

Knock, knock. (Pretend to knock on door.) Joseph knocked on the wooden door.

"May we have a room for the night?" Joseph asked the innkeeper.

"I'm sorry," said the innkeeper. "There is no room." *(Shake head no.)*

"But we have traveled a long way," said Joseph. "Is there no place for us in all of Bethlehem?"

The innkeeper looked at Joseph. He looked at Mary. "Well, there is a stable behind the inn," he said. "It is warm, and the animals are friendly."

Clippity clop, clippity clop. (Pat legs.) Mary and Joseph led the donkey inside the stable.

M-a-ah, m-a-ah. M-o-o, m-o-o. Joseph heard the sounds of the goat and cow as he fed the donkey.

C-o-o, c-o-o. Mary heard the soft sound of the doves as she rested on the sweet-smelling hay. It was quiet in the stable except for the gentle sounds of the animals. Before long there was another sound in the stable.

W-a-a, w-a-a. It was the cry of a newborn baby. Baby Jesus was born!

"I love you, baby Jesus," said Mary. *(Have the children repeat.)* She wrapped the tiny baby in soft bands of cloth. The cloth would help baby Jesus feel safe and warm.

"I love you, baby Jesus," said Joseph. *(Have the children repeat.)* He filled the animals' feed box with fresh hay. The hay would make a soft bed for the tiny baby.

Mary sang softly as she rocked her new baby boy to sleep. *(Pretend to rock baby.)* Then she laid baby Jesus in his manger bed.

Joseph smiled as the sound of Mary's singing drifted through the still night air.

Based on Luke 2:1-7.

Jesus Is Born

by Sharilyn S. Adair

Pretend to be Mary. Ask the children to repeat after you the phrases that are in boldface type. Teach them some signal, such as cupping your hand to your ear, that you will give just before you say the phrase they are to repeat.

What a lovely night it is in Bethlehem! The stars are shining, and the night feels warm but not too hot—**just right for a tiny baby.**

Joseph and I traveled all day. **We walked and walked.** When we came to town, we were so tired. **We wanted to lie down and rest.**

We went to many houses. Joseph knocked on their doors. At each place he asked, **"Do you have room for us?"**

"No, no!" said the people. "We are full." I was sad and afraid that we would not find a place to sleep.

Finally Joseph found us a warm stable where we could spend the night. The hay smells fresh and sweet—**just right for a tiny baby.**

And something wonderful has happened! Now there are three of us—there is me, there is Joseph, and **now there is baby Jesus.**

Baby Jesus is tiny and cuddly. **I wrapped him in soft cloths.** Then I found a warm, clean place where he could sleep. The box where the animals get their food was **just right for a tiny baby.** I rocked baby Jesus and sang to him. **Then I laid him in the manger.** Shh! He's sleeping now. I'm going to sleep too. *(Lay head in hands and pretend to go to sleep.)*

Based on Luke 2:1-7.

Good News! Clap! Clap!

by Elizabeth Crocker

Good news! Clap, clap!
(Clap hands twice.)
Good news! Tap, tap!
(Stomp feet twice.)
Christmas Day is near.
(Make a "C" with your right hand. Move the "C" in an arc in front of your body. This is sign language for Christmas.)

Good news! Clap, clap!
(Clap hands twice.)
Good news! Tap, tap!
(Stomp feet twice.)
Listen to me cheer!
(Cup hands around mouth.)

Good news! Clap, clap!
(Clap hands twice.)
Good news! Tap, tap!
(Stomp feet twice.)
Mary has a son.
(Pretend to rock baby Jesus in your arms.)

Good news! Clap, clap!
(Clap hands twice.)
Good news! Tap, tap!
(Stomp feet twice.)
God loves us everyone.
(Hug yourself.)

Based on Luke 2.

Five Little Shepherds

by Daphna Flegal

Five little shepherds watching their sheep.
(Hold up hand and wiggle fingers.)
The first one said: "It's time to sleep."
(Hold up one finger.)
The second one said: "Wait, do you see
that light?"
(Hold up two fingers.)
The third one said: "It shines very bright!"
(Hold up three fingers)
The fourth one said: "I hear angels sing."
(Hold up four fingers.)
The fifth one said: "Let's go see the tiny king."
(Hold up five fingers.)
Five little shepherds hurried on their way
To see baby Jesus born this day.
(Wiggle fingers.)

Based on Luke 2:8-20.

Shepherds Visit Jesus

Tell this story using the sheep, shepherd, angel and baby Jesus finger puppets (see instructions at right). Let the children make the three sheep finger puppets. Help the children put the sheep finger puppets on three fingers of one hand. Encourage the children to hold up their finger puppets as you count **"one, two, three"** and repeat the sound **"baa! baa!"** each time you say the words in the story.

Before telling the story, place the sheep finger puppets on one of your hands and the shepherd, angel, and baby Jesus finger puppets on the other hand. Keep the fingers with the angel and baby Jesus finger puppets turned down until they are mentioned in the story.

One, two, three," counted the shepherds. The shepherds were counting their sheep. *(Hold up the shepherd finger puppet and three sheep puppets. Have the children hold up their three sheep finger puppets as you count.)*

"Baa! Baa!" said the sheep. *(Children repeat sheep sounds.)* The sheep followed the shepherds.

"One, two, three," said the shepherds. *(Hold up the shepherd finger puppet and three sheep puppets. Have the children hold up their three sheep finger puppets as you count.)*

The shepherds were taking the sheep to a place to rest for the night. The shepherds wanted to make sure that all the sheep were safe.

"Baa! Baa!" said the sheep. *(Children repeat sheep sounds.)* Soon all the sheep were safe for the night. *(Place hand with sheep finger puppets in lap.)*

While the sheep were resting, one shepherd played music on a flute. *"Twooo-twooo-whooo,"* went the flute.

Suddenly the shepherd stopped playing the flute. The shepherds saw an angel, and they were afraid. *(Hold up angel puppet.)*

"Do not be afraid," said the angel. "I am bringing good news of great joy. On this night in Bethlehem Jesus is born. You will find the baby Jesus wrapped in soft cloths and lying in a manger."

Some of the shepherds went to Bethlehem to see baby Jesus. One shepherd carried a lamb in his arms. *(Hold up one sheep finger puppet and have the children hold up one of their sheep puppets.)*

"Baa, baa," said the little lamb. *(Children repeat sheep sounds.)*

In Bethlehem they found baby Jesus in a manger just as the angel had said. *(Hold up baby Jesus puppet.)*

The shepherds were happy. When they left, the shepherds told others, "Jesus is born! Jesus is born!"

"Baa, baa," said the little sheep. *(Children hold up one sheep finger puppet and repeat sheep sounds.)*

Based on Luke 2:8-20.

Make Shepherd, Angel, and Baby Jesus Finger Puppets

Supplies: scissors, tape

Directions

• Copy the shepherd, angel, and baby Jesus finger puppets. Cut apart the puppets. Fold the finger puppets along the dotted lines. Tape the sides of the finger puppets together.

Make Sheep Finger Puppets

Supplies: scissors, tape, glue, cotton balls

Directions

• Copy the three sheep finger puppets for each child. Cut apart the puppets. Write each child's name on the puppets.
• Let each child glue a cotton ball onto each sheep finger puppet.
• Help each child fold the finger puppets along the dotted lines. Tape the sides of the finger puppets together.
• Help each child put the sheep finger puppets on his or her fingers.

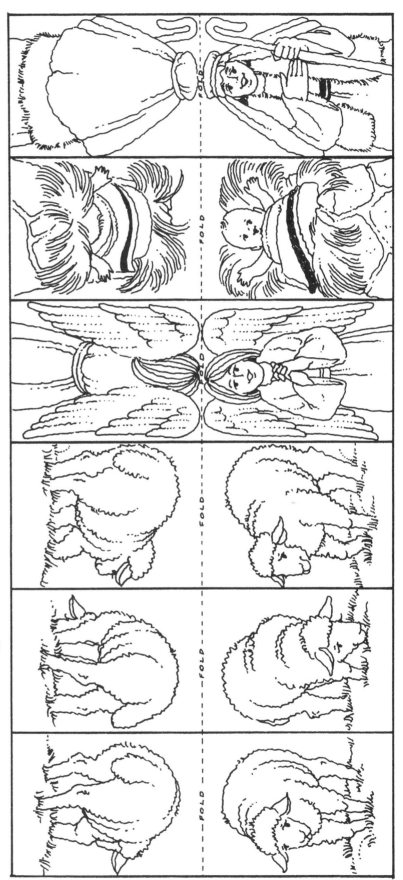

Twinkle, Twinkle, Twinkle
by Susan Isbell

Twinkle, twinkle, twinkle,
(Hold hands over head.)

Stars of Christmas Day.
(Flutter fingers.)

Merry Christmas, Merry Christmas,
This is what they say.

Look, a Star
by Susan Isbell

Have the children hold up one of their arms and wiggle their fingers each time you say **"Twinkle, twinkle."** Or let the children make star poles to use with the poem (see instructions at right). Encourage the children to wave their star poles in the air each time you say the words **"Twinkle, twinkle."**

Look, there's a star shining in the night.
Twinkle, twinkle, such a pretty sight.
Look, there are the wise men coming from afar.
Twinkle, twinkle, they're following the star.
Look, there's the mother with her special boy.
Twinkle, twinkle, the star shines bright
with joy.

Based on Matthew 2:1-11.

Make Star Poles

Supplies: scissors, crayons or glitter crayons, small paper plates, glue, tape, craft sticks

Directions

• Copy the star circle for each child. Cut out the circles for younger children. Give each child a star circle.

• Let the children color the stars with crayons or glitter crayons.

• Give each child a small paper plate. Let the children glue their star circles onto the paper plates. Glue or tape a craft stick onto the back of the paper plate.

• Show the children how to hold their star poles by the craft sticks.

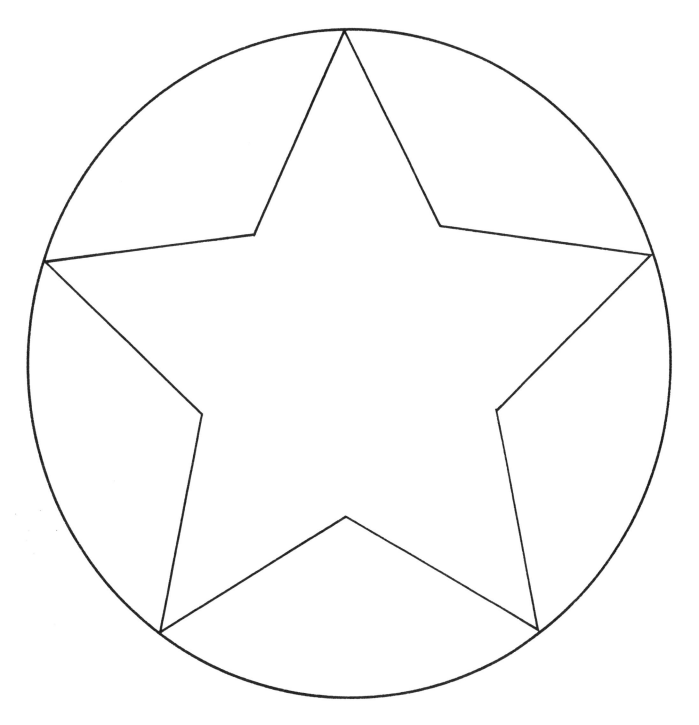

Wise Men Visit Jesus

Use the star pole (page 65) as you tell this story. Or use a star Christmas tree ornament. Begin in one corner of your room. Hold up the star.

Say: Follow the star around the room as I tell you a story about three wise men.

Tell the first part of the story. Then hold up the star and have the children follow you to another part of your room. Stop and tell the next part of the story. Continue until you have finished the story.

Look!" said the first wise man. "Look up in the sky!" (*Hold up the star pole.*)

"A star!" said the second wise man. "It is the brightest star I have ever seen."

"We must follow the star," said the third wise man. "It will lead us to the new king."

"We must take the new king gifts," said the first wise man. "Gifts of gold, frankincense, and myrrh."

The wise men packed their gifts and other things they needed for the trip on camels.

(*Hold up the star pole and lead the children to another part of the room. Have the children move like camels each time you say* **"Harump! Harump!"**)

Harump! Harump! The wise men rode their camels and followed the star.

(*Hold up the star pole and lead the children to another part of the room.*)

Harump! Harump! The wise men rode their camels to find the new king.

(*Hold up the star pole and lead the children to another part of the room.*)

Harump! Harump! The wise men rode their camels to Bethlehem.

(*Hold up the star pole and lead the children to another part of the room. Stay here to finish the story.*)

"Look, the star has stopped!" said the first wise man.

"Let's go into the house!" said the third wise man. When the wise men entered the house, they saw Jesus and his mother, Mary. The wise men knelt near Jesus and gave him their gifts of gold, frankincense, and myrrh. Jesus was the new king!

Based on Matthew 2:1-11.
© 1994 Cokesbury.

Three Wise Men
by Elizabeth Crocker

Three wise men traveled far,
(*Hold up three fingers.*)
Following a big, bright star.
(*Hold other hand above head with palm out, fingers extended to be the star.*)

The first one said, "Look how it glows!"
(*Hold up one finger.*)
The second one said, "Look where it goes!"
(*Hold up two fingers.*)
The third one said, "It shines so bright,
(*Hold up three fingers.*)
I know we'll find the king tonight!"

Three wise men traveled far
(*Wiggle three fingers.*)
Following a big, bright star.
(*Hold other hand above head with palm out, fingers extended to be the star.*)

Based on Matthew 2:1-11.
© 1994 Cokesbury.

Jesus Grows

Just Like Me and You!

Jesus learned things as he grew.
(Crouch down, then stand up.)
Just like me,
(Point to self.)
And just like you!
(Point to others.)
He learned to walk,
(Walk in place.)
And run and jump,
(Run in place; jump in place.)
He learned to stand up tall.
*(Stretch up on tiptoes;
raise arms above head.)*
He learned to talk,
(Point to mouth.)
And laugh and sing,
*(Fold arms over stomach,
shake arms as if saying ha, ha, ha;
cup hands around mouth.)*
He learned God loves us all.
(Hug self.)
God loved Jesus as he grew.
(Crouch down, then stand up.)
Just like me,
(Point to self.)
And just like you!
(Point to others.)

Based on Luke 2:40.

Jesus Grew

Jesus grew from a baby,
(Rock baby in your arms.)
just like me and you.
(Point to self, point to others.)
He learned to walk.
(Walk in place.)
He learned to talk.
(Cup hands around mouth.)
He grew and grew and grew!
*(Crouch down, then stretch up slowly
to tiptoes with arms overhead.)*

Based on Luke 2:40.

Jesus Learns

Have the children do motions for the following words:

Step, step, step: *walk in place.*
Listen, listen, listen: *put a hand to one ear.*
Look, look, look: *put a hand above eyes.*

Step, step, step. Everyone walked on the road that led to Jerusalem.

Step, step, step. Fathers walked.

Step, step, step. So did the children.

Mary, Joseph, and Jesus were in the crowd. They were all going to the Temple to learn about God.

Step, step, step. It was a long trip.

Listen, listen, listen. Everyone was glad to go to the Temple. Joseph, Mary, and Jesus sat in the Temple and heard the teachers. They heard the teachers pray and talk about God.

Step, step, step. Soon it was time to go. Everyone except Jesus left the Temple and traveled back home.

Listen, listen, listen. Jesus did not leave with his mother and father and the other people. Jesus stayed and listened to the teachers. He asked the teachers questions about God.

Look, look, look. While Jesus was in the Temple, Mary and Joseph looked for him. They did not know where Jesus was. Finally they found Jesus in the Temple with the teachers.

"We have been looking for you," said Mary. "We were worried."

"Didn't you know I would be in the Temple learning about God?" asked Jesus.

Step, step, step. Jesus, Mary, and Joseph went home to Nazareth. Jesus learned about God as he grew.

Based on Luke 2:41-52.

Jesus Is Baptized

Give each child blue crepe paper streamers, ribbons, or recycled streamers (see below) to be water streamers. Have the children move the water streamers made in class each time you say the word **water**.

The cool *water* splashed along the river's bank. This *water* was from the Jordan River. The river was wide, but in some places the *water* flowed in small streams. A man named John used this *water* in the Jordan River to baptize people. John also told the people about Jesus.

One day Jesus saw John baptizing people in the cool *water*. Jesus wanted John to baptize him too. So Jesus stepped carefully into the *water*, and John baptized him. After Jesus was baptized, a dove appeared, and God said some special words about Jesus. "You are my son, and I am pleased with you," God said.

Then Jesus stepped out of the *water*. Jesus was glad that John baptized him.

Based on Luke 3:21-22.

Make Recycled Streamers

• Cut legs from clean nylon pantyhose or order waste pantyhose from L'Eggs. Let the children use the pantyhose like streamers.

• Nylon waste pantyhose is available from L'Eggs. Send a request letter and $10 per box to:

Peggy Oates
Sara Lee Hosiery - L'Eggs Products
P.O. Box 719, Florence, SC 29571.

• Make checks payable to Sara Lee Hosiery and mark "For waste hose." Each box contains about 300 waste pantyhose. Price is subject to change without notice.

• The pantyhose may be dyed using fabric dyes.

God's Dear Son

by Elizabeth Crocker

Have the children repeat the words **"Spla-a-s-s-sh, spla-a-s-s-sh"** after you. Let the children make rippling motions with their fingers to represent water.

Spla-a-s-s-sh, spla-a-s-s-sh. The water felt cool against John's skin. John was in the Jordan River, telling the people about God and baptizing them. People had been coming all day.

Spla-a-s-s-sh, spla-a-s-s-sh. Jesus felt the water splashing against his feet as he walked to the edge of the river.

"I am here to be baptized," Jesus told John.

"Jesus," said John, "I should be baptized by you." John knew that Jesus loved God very much.

"John, this is what God wants us to do," said Jesus. Spla-a-s-s-sh, spla-a-s-s-sh. Jesus walked into the river and stood next to John.

Spla-a-s-s-sh, spla-a-s-s-sh. John baptized Jesus with the water.

After Jesus was baptized, a dove appeared, and Jesus heard God's voice. "This is my own dear son," God said. "I am pleased with him."

Spla-a-s-s-sh, spla-a-s-s-sh. Jesus felt the cool water of the river swirling around him. Jesus knew that God was with him, and that God loved him very much.

Based on Matthew 3:13-17.

Followers of Jesus

Jesus Called Four Fishermen
by Joyce Stenberg

"Throw the net into the lake," Peter told his brother Andrew. They tossed the large, heavy net into the water. *(Pretend to throw the net.)* "There. Now we have to sit quietly and wait for the fish to swim into the net." *(Sit quietly and pretend to watch for fish.)*

When the net was full, the brothers pulled in the heavy net and put the fish into large baskets. *(Pretend to pull in the heavy net.)*

"Let's throw the net into the lake again, Andrew," said Peter. "Here we go," Andrew shouted. *(Pretend to throw the net.)*

Just then they looked up and saw Jesus walking along the shore. *(Walk in place, then stop.)* Jesus saw Peter and Andrew fishing and called to them, "Peter, Andrew, follow me. I will show you how to fish for people." *(Repeat Jesus' words and motion to the disciples to come.)*

At once Peter and Andrew left their nets and went with Jesus. *(Pretend to pull nets in and drop them on the ground.)* As Jesus and Peter and Andrew walked along the lake, they saw James and John. *(Walk in place again and stop.)*

"James, John, follow me. I will show you how to fish for people," Jesus called. *(Repeat Jesus'* words and motion to the disciples to come.)* James and John quickly left their nets and went with Jesus. *(Pretend to put nets down and walk in place.)*

"We will follow you, Jesus," Peter, Andrew, James, and John said. *(Repeat what the disciples said.)*

Based on Matthew 4:18-22.
© 1996 Cokesbury.

Stand Up and Walk
by Joyce Riffe

Here is the man upon his mat,
Not moving foot or hand.
(Lie still.)
Then Jesus said, "Stand up and walk."
The man rose up to stand.
(Slowly stand up.)
He smiled at Jesus happily.
(Smile.)
He rolled his mat away.
(Pantomime rolling mat.)
He smiled at others in the crowd,
(Smile.)
And then walked home that day.
(Walk in a circle.)

Based on Matthew 9:1-7.
© 1996 Cokesbury.

The Special Ointment

by Daphna Flegal

Use sweet-smelling air freshener or perfume (see directions at right) as you tell this story.

Martha," Mary called to her sister. "Jesus is almost here. I can see him walking with his friends."

"I have supper ready," answered Martha. "They will be hungry after their long, dusty walk."

"I wish I could think of a way to show Jesus how happy I am he is our friend," said Mary.

"You can help me serve supper," replied Martha.

Mary smiled. Martha always wanted help. But Mary wanted to do something special for Jesus. Then she remembered the ointment. It had cost a lot of money. But that did not matter. She would use it to show Jesus how important he was to her.

"I am glad to sit and rest with my friends," said Jesus as he ate the supper Martha had cooked for him.

Mary went to Jesus. She held the ointment in her hands. Quietly she knelt at his feet.

"You are tired from your walk," Mary said to Jesus. "Your feet are dusty and hot. Let me cool them."

Jesus nodded to Mary. She rubbed the ointment on his feet. The ointment felt cool and soothing. It had a wonderful smell that filled the whole house. Everyone could smell the ointment. The smell told them that the ointment was special. Everyone knew that Mary thought Jesus was even more special than the ointment.

Based on John 12:1-8.

Directions
• Purchase a sweet-smelling air freshener jar (some are available in little clay pots that look similar to a Bible-times jar). Or pour a small amount of perfume on a cotton ball. Place the cotton ball in a small paper cup.

• Have the children sit in a circle.

• **Say: People in Bible times liked to use sweet-smelling ointment.**

• Pass the jar or cup around the circle and encourage the children to smell the perfume.

• Set the jar or cup in the center of the circle and then tell the children the story "The Special Ointment."

At the Well
by Daphna Flegal

Jesus walked and walked.
(Walk in place.)
He walked to a city.
(Walk in place.)
The sun was shining.
(Make a circle with arms, hold overhead.)
It was very hot.
(Wipe brow.)
Jesus saw a well.
(Point in the distance.)
There was water in the well.
(Wave hands to make water.)

Jesus was thirsty.
(Wipe hand across mouth.)
He was tired.
(Sigh and shrug shoulders.)
Jesus sat down by the well.
(Crouch down.)

A woman walked and walked.
(Walk in place.)
She walked to the well.
(Walk in place.)
She was carrying a water jar.
(Pretend to hold jar while walking in place.)
The woman stopped at the well to get water.
(Stop walking.)

"Give me a drink," said Jesus.
(Hold out hand.)
The woman was surprised.
(Hold up hands as if surprised.)
She didn't think Jesus would talk to her.
(Shake head no.)

But Jesus did talk to her.
(Shake head yes.)
He talked to her about water.
(Cup hand and pretend to drink.)
He talked to her about the things she had done.
(Place hands on hips.)
He talked to her about God's love.
(Hold hands over heart.)

The woman was very happy.
(Point to smile.)
She ran to tell others about Jesus.
(Run in place.)
Jesus taught the others about God's love for everyone.
(Hold hands over heart.)

Based on John 4:5-26, 28-30.
© 1997 Cokesbury.

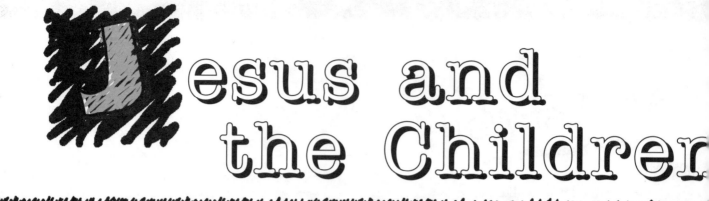

Jesus and the Children

The Little Children Came

by Joyce Riffe

Have the children do the motions and repeat the phrase, **"The little children came."**

Jesus said, "Come near me."
(Motion "come here" with hand.)
The little children came.
Jesus said, "Sit by my knee."
(Pat knees.)
The little children came.
Jesus smiled and hugged them too.
(Hug self.)
The little children came.
Jesus told them, "God loves you."
(Point to self.)
The little children came.

Based on Mark 10:13-16.

To See Jesus

by Daphna Flegal

Bible people brought their children
to see Jesus.
The children walked, walked, walked
to see Jesus.
(Walk in place.)

Bible people brought their children to see Jesus.
The children marched, marched, marched
to see Jesus.
(March in place.)

Bible people brought their children to see Jesus.
The children jumped, jumped, jumped
to see Jesus.
(Jump in place.)

Bible people brought their children to see Jesus.
The children hopped, hopped, hopped
to see Jesus.
(Hop on one foot.)

Bible people brought their children to see Jesus.
The children tiptoed, tiptoed, tiptoed
to see Jesus.
(Tiptoe.)

Based on Mark 10:13-16.

Happy to See Jesus

by Daphna Flegal

Step. Step. Step. *(Pat knees.)* The children and their fathers stepped on the path leading to the hillside. They were going to see Jesus.

Skip. Skip. Skip. *(Clap hands.)* The children and their mothers skipped up the path to the hillside. They were going to see Jesus.

Look. Look. Look. *(Put hand above eyes.)* The children and their mothers saw a large number of people crowded around Jesus. Everyone wanted to see Jesus.

Push. Push. Push. *(Push hands away from body.)* The children and their fathers tried to push their way through the large crowd of people. They wanted to get close to Jesus.

"Stop," said one of the men. *(Hold up one hand.)* "We are trying to hear what Jesus has to say."

"We have brought our children to see Jesus," said one mother.

"Jesus does not have time for children," said another man. *(Shake head no.)* "Take your children home."

Turn. Turn. Turn. *(Turn around.)* The children turned to go away.

"Wait," said Jesus. "Let the little children come to me. Do not stop them." *(Motion "come here" with hand.)*

Run. Run. Run. *(Pat knees quickly.)* One child ran happily to Jesus. Then another child ran to Jesus. Then another and another and another.

Talk. Talk. Talk. *(Move hands near mouth to indicate talking.)* Soon there were many children gathered around Jesus. They were all talking to Jesus. Jesus touched each child.

"God loves you," said Jesus to each child. "You are important to God."

Smile. Smile. Smile. *(Point to smile.)* The children were happy to see Jesus.

Based on Mark 10:13-16.

Going to See Jesus

Five little children
Went happily on their way.
(Hold up five fingers.)
They were going to see Jesus,
to laugh and talk and play.
(Wiggle fingers.)
The first little child
came running for a hug.
(Hold up one finger.)
The second little child
took time to watch a bug.
(Hold up two fingers.)
The third little child
held his mother's hand so tight.
(Hold up three fingers.)
The fourth little child
laughed loudly with delight.
(Hold up four fingers.)
The fifth little child
brought a handful of flowers.
(Hold up five fingers.)
The five little children
stayed and talked for hours.
(Wiggle fingers.)
Five little children came to hear Jesus say,
"Let the children come to me,
do not send them away."

Based on Mark 10:13-16.

Here Come the Children
by Daphna Flegal

Here come the children one by one.
(Hold up one finger.)
Some like to walk, some like to run.
(Walk in place; run in place.)
God loves children one by one.
(Hold up one finger.)

Here come the children two by two.
(Hold up two fingers.)
Some have brown eyes, some have blue.
(Point to eyes.)
God loves children two by two.
(Hold up two fingers.)

Here come the children three by three.
(Hold up three fingers.)
Some look like you, some like me.
(Point to others, point to self.)
God loves children three by three.
(Hold up three fingers.)

Here come the children four by four.
(Hold up four fingers.)
Some live far away, some next door.
(Sweep arms away from body;
bring arms back close to body.)
God loves children four by four.
(Hold up four fingers.)

Here come the children five by five.
(Hold up five fingers.)
Every age and every size.
(Pretend to pat heads
of different-sized children.)
God loves children five by five.
(Hold up five fingers.)

Here come more children for you to see.
(Hold up five fingers on other hand.)
Each one is special, I know you'll agree.
(Wiggle all ten fingers.)
For God loves all children, and God loves me!
(Hug self.)

Based on Mark 10:13-16.

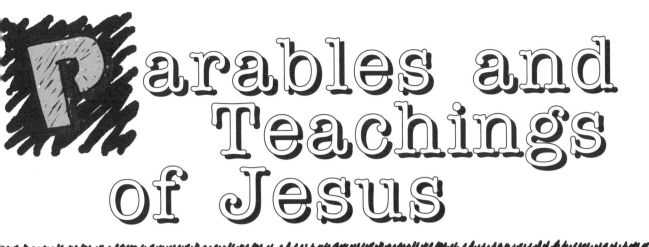

Parables and Teachings of Jesus

Who Is My Neighbor?

by Susan Isbell

Show the children how to pat their thighs in an alternating pattern to make walking and running sounds.

You should love your neighbor as you love yourself," said the man listening to Jesus.

"Yes," said Jesus. "You are right."

"But who is our neighbor?" asked the man. Jesus told this story:

A man was walking down a rocky road. *(Pat thighs to make walking sound.)*

Suddenly robbers came out from behind the rocks. *(Abruptly stop patting thighs.)* They hurt the man and took all of his money. Then the robbers ran away and left the man alone. *(Pat thighs quickly to make running sound.)*

Soon a priest from the Temple came walking down the same road. *(Pat thighs to make walking sound.)* He saw the hurt man.

"Please help me," said the hurt man.

The priest could tell the man needed help, but he was afraid to stop. *What if the robbers are still nearby?* he thought to himself. The priest did not stop to help. He crossed to the other side of the road and hurried on his way. *(Pat thighs quickly to make running sound.)*

Later in the day a second man came walking down the road. *(Pat thighs to make walking sound.)*

"Please help me," said the hurt man.

But the second man did not stop to help. He crossed to the other side of the road and hurried on his way. *(Pat thighs quickly to make running sound.)*

Then a third man came riding down the road on his donkey. This man was called a Samaritan. *(Pat floor or bottom of chair to make sound of donkey walking.)*

"Please help me," said the hurt man.
The Samaritan stopped to help. *(Stop patting floor or chair.)* He carefully put the man onto his donkey and led him to a place where he could rest and get better. The Samaritan even paid for the hurt man's care. *(Pat floor or bottom of chair to make sound of donkey walking.)*

Jesus finished the story and asked, "Three men walked down the road and saw the hurt man. Which of the three men do you think was a neighbor to the hurt man?

Which of the three men do you think was a good neighbor?

Based on Luke 10:25-37.

The Lost Sheep
by Susan Isbell

"**B**aa! Baa!" The sheep followed the shepherd up the grassy hill. (*Have the children pretend to be sheep. Lead the pretend sheep to the story area.*)

"*Baa! Baa!*" It was almost night. The shepherd led the sheep to a safe place to sleep. (*Have the children sit down in your story area.*)

"*Baa! Baa!*" The shepherd counted his sheep. The shepherd knew there were one hundred sheep in his flock. (*Count your children, touching them on the head as you count.*)

"Ninety-seven. Ninety-eight. Ninety-nine." The shepherd counted his sheep again. One sheep was missing!

The shepherd gathered the ninety-nine sheep together and set out to find the one that was lost. He searched the fields. He searched the caves. He searched the bushes. (*Walk among the children seated in your story area. Pretend to look for the lost sheep.*)

"*Baa-aa! Baa-aa!*" Then the shepherd heard the sound of one frightened sheep. The shepherd ran toward the sound. There, under a bush, was the one lost sheep! (*Choose one child to be the lost sheep. Touch the child on the head.*)

"Yea!" shouted the shepherd. He carefully picked up the sheep in his arms and brought it back to the flock. (*Have the lost sheep stand up.*)

"*Baa! Baa!*" (*Whisper.*) Soon all one hundred sheep were resting for the night. (*Have all the children pretend to sleep.*)

The shepherd was very happy. He called his friends and neighbors together to tell them the good news.

"I found my sheep!" he said to everyone. "I found my sheep!"

Based on Luke 15:1-6.
© 1994 Cokesbury.

Five Little Sheep
by Sandra Jaimison

Five little sheep, all in a flock.
(*Hold up five fingers; wiggle them.*)
Some like to run; some like to walk.
(*Move fingers forward; then back towards you.*)
Here is the shepherd, counting his sheep.
(*Hold up one finger on other hand,*
touch each finger on first hand as if counting sheep.)
He feeds them, loves them,
and sings them to sleep.
(*Clasp both hands together, bring to chest.*)

Continue the finger play, changing five sheep to four sheep, then three sheep, then two sheep, holding up the appropriate number of fingers as each verse is said. When you get to one sheep, change to the following verse:

One little sheep, not with the flock.
(*Hold up one finger; wiggle it.*)
Did he run? Did he walk?
(*Move finger forward; then back toward you.*)
Here is the shepherd, looking for his sheep.
(*Hold up finger on other hand.*)
He finds him, loves him, and sings him to sleep.
(*Clasp both hands together, bring to chest.*)

Based on Luke 15:1-6.
Copyright © 1994 Cokesbury

The Loving Father
by Susan Isbell

Have the children do motions to the following words:

Happy: *applaud.*
Sad: *rub eyes as if crying.*

Once upon a time there was a man who had two sons that he loved very much. The two sons made the man very **happy**.

One day the younger son came to the father and said, "I am tired of living at home. Give me my share of the family money now. I want to leave home." The father must have felt **sad**, but he gave the young son the money.

The son was excited. He went to a country far, far away. He spent lots of money! He had lots of fun! He was **happy!**

But soon all his money was gone. He had no money for food. Alone and **sad**, the son finally found a job.

Oink! Oink! His job was feeding pigs. And he hated pigs! He didn't even want to touch the pigs. But he was so hungry, he would be glad to eat the pigs' food. The son was very **sad.**

The son decided to go home. He wanted to tell his father he was sorry. He hoped his father would give him a job working in the fields. The son went back to his home. As he came near his house, he could not believe what he saw. His father was running down the road to meet him! The son was very **happy!**

"My son!" cried the father. "My son is home!" His father hugged him, kissed him, and welcomed him home. The father was very **happy!**

"Father, I'm sorry," said the son. "I have no money left. I made a mistake. What I did was wrong." The son felt **sad**.

"I love you, and I'm glad you are home," said the father.

The father planned a big party to welcome his son home. The father and the son were **happy.**

Jesus told this story so that people would know that God loves and forgives each of us, even when we make mistakes and do something wrong. Making mistakes can make us **sad**, but God's love can make us **happy.**

Based on Luke 15:1-3, 11-24.

The Lost Son

by Susan Isbell

Here is a story. Let's listen and see
How it tells of God's love for you and me.
*(Hold up the finger puppets on one hand.
Use the other hand to point to each puppet.)*
Here is the father who loved his two sons.
(Point to the puppet that shows the father.)
Here is the son who left home to find fun.
*(Point to the puppet that shows
the son holding a bag of money.)*
Here is the pig the son fed every day.
(Point to the puppet that shows the pig.)
Here is the son going back home to say:
"Father, I'm sorry, what I did was wrong."
(Point to the puppet of the son on his knees.)
Here is the father who loved all along.
*(Point to the puppet that shows
the father hugging the son.)*
Jesus told this story about father and son.
So we'd know that God loves us,
each and every one.

Based on Luke 15:11-32.
© 1996 Cokesbury.

Make Lost Son Finger Puppets
Supplies: scissors, crayons, tape, glue

Directions
• Copy the finger puppets and pig shape for each child. Cut apart the puppets and pig. Let the children decorate the pig shape with crayons. Write each child's name on the pig.

• Show the children how to fold the pigs along the dotted line. Tape or glue the sides of the pigs together, leaving the top open to make envelopes.

• Give each child the finger puppets. Help each child fold the puppets along the dotted lines. Tape the sides of the puppets together.

• Help the children put their puppets on one hand. Put a set on your own hand. Say the fingerplay for your children. Use your free hand to point to each puppet.

• Have the children put their finger puppets inside their envelopes to take home.

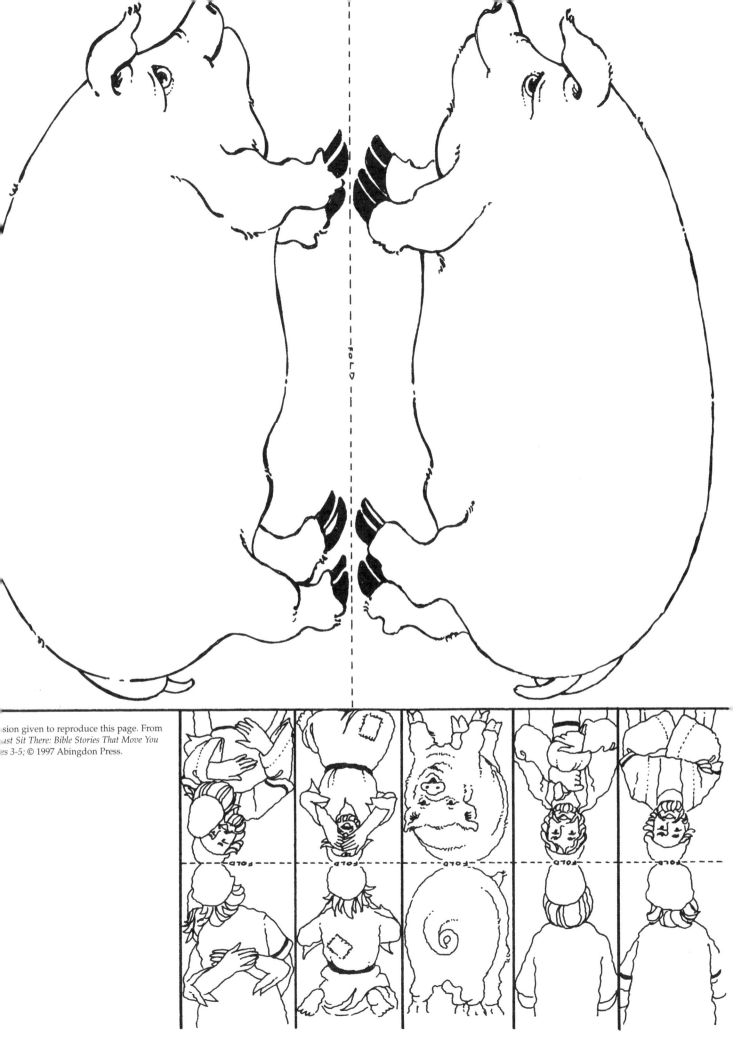

Teach Us to Pray

by Daphna Flegal

"**D**ear God, thank you for this food," Jesus prayed before he shared some bread and fish with his friends. *(Fold hands in prayer.)*

"Dear God, help me make this man well," Jesus prayed before he helped a man who was sick. *(Cross arms over chest.)*

"Dear God, help me do what you want me to do," Jesus prayed before he went to sleep at night. *(Raise arms up.)*

Jesus' friends noticed Jesus praying. *(Fold hands in prayer.)* They noticed that every time he taught the people or helped someone, Jesus prayed to God. *(Cross arms over chest.)* Jesus' friends loved him, and they wanted to be like him.

"Jesus," said his friends, "teach us to pray." *(Raise arms up.)*

Jesus was happy his friends wanted to learn how to pray. He knew that prayer was very important to God. So Jesus gave his friends a special prayer to say.

"Pray this way," said Jesus. *(Fold hands in prayer.)*

---

*O*ur Father in heaven,
　hallowed be your name,
　your kingdom come,
　your will be done,
　　on earth as in heaven.
　Give us today our daily bread.
　Forgive us our sins
　　as we forgive those who sin against us.
　Save us from the time of trial,
　　and deliver us from evil.
　For the kingdom, the power, and the
　　glory are yours now and for ever.
　Amen.

Based on Matthew 6:9-13.

© 1995 Cokesbury.

The Lord's Prayer is the English translation of *The Lord's Prayer* by the International Consultation on English Texts. From *The United Methodist Hymnal,* 894.

Copyright © 1995 Cokesbury.

Jesus Teaches Us to Pray

by Sue Downing

The disciples talked with Jesus one day.
*(Move fingers of both hands
in an open/shut motion.)*
Please, Lord, teach us
(Point to self.)
How to pray.
(Fold hands in prayer.)

Jesus showed his loving care
(Cross hands over heart.)
By praying with them a special prayer.
(Fold hands in prayer.)
Jesus also gives
(Extend arms outward.)
This prayer
(Fold hands in prayer.)
For me and you.
(Point to self and others.)
For we can learn from Jesus too!
(Extend outsretched arms upward.)

Based on Matthew 6:9-13.

Easter

Shout Hosanna!
by Joyce Riffe

Jesus rode a donkey into the city. Crowds of people welcomed him. Some people laid their coats on the road in front of the donkey. Other people cut leafy branches and waved the branches high in the air.

"Hosanna! Hosanna!" cried the people. "Welcome, Jesus!"

You can act out this story with the following action poem:

Here comes Jesus! Here comes Jesus!
Riding down the street.
(Put hands above eyes as if looking into distance.)

Everyone, take off your coat,
And lay it at his feet.
(Pretend to take off coat, lay it on the floor.)

Everyone, wave branches green,
All along the way.
(Pretend to wave branches.)

Shout "Hosanna!"
Shout "Hosanna!"
On this happy day.
(Shout "Hosanna!")

Based on Matthew 21:1-11; Mark 11:9.
© 1995 Cokesbury.

Little Donkey
by Joyce Riffe

Have the children sit down. Show the children how to pat their legs to make the sound of the donkey walking. Keep the rhythm going as you say the poem.

Little donkey
In the street,
Cloaks and robes
About his feet.
Branches green
Waved overhead,
Words of welcome
Loudly said,
Carried Jesus
Carefully,
Slow and sure
For all to see.

Based on Matthew 21:1-11; Mark 11:9.
© 1996 Cokesbury.

Hosanna, Shout Hosanna!

by Daphna Flegal

Give each child a real palm branch or a paper palm branch (see p. 86). Encourage the children to wave their palm branches as instructed in the poem. Or have each child hold up one arm to be the palm branch.

Hosanna, shout hosanna!
Wave your palm branches high.
(Wave palm branch up high.)
Hosanna, shout hosanna!
Can you touch the sky?
(Reach above head with palm branch.)

Hosanna, shout hosanna!
Now wave your palm branch low.
(Wave palm branch down low.)
Hosanna, shout hosanna!
Can you turn around real slow?
(Turn around slowly.)

Hosanna, shout hosanna!
Now lay your palm branch down.
(Lay palm branch on the floor.)
Hosanna, shout hosanna!
Can you march to town?
(March in place.)

Hosanna, shout hosanna!
Welcome Jesus on this day.
(Clap hands.)
Hosanna, shout hosanna!
Can you hear me say . . .
(Cup hands around ear.)
"Hosanna, shout hosanna!"

Based on Matthew 21:1-11; Mark 11:9.
© 1996 Cokesbury.

© 1996 Cokesbury.

Hosanna! Here Comes Jesus!

by Susan Isbell

Give each child a real palm branch or a paper palm branch (see directions at right). Encourage the children to wave their palm branches and say **"Hosanna! Hosanna!"** each time it appears in the story.

"**G**o into the next town," Jesus said to two of his disciples. "There you will find a donkey. Bring the donkey to me so that I can ride it into town."

The two disciples did as Jesus asked. The owner of the donkey was happy to let Jesus ride the donkey into Jerusalem. Someone threw a coat over the donkey's back. Jesus climbed on. Jesus rode the donkey into a city called Jerusalem.

As Jesus came closer to the city, the people began to shout. **"Hosanna! Hosanna!"** they cheered. "Blessed is the one who comes in the name of the Lord!"

Someone broke a branch from a palm tree and began to wave it as Jesus passed. More people broke branches from trees and began to shout, **"Hosanna! Hosanna!"** They waved their branches and cheered. Everyone was happy to see Jesus.

Jesus rode slowly down the crowded street. From the doorways he heard people shout, **"Hosanna! Hosanna!"**

Children everywhere began to wave branches and run alongside the donkey. The children began to shout, **"Hosanna! Hosanna!"**

The donkey moved steadily down the street. Some people took off their coats and tossed them across the dusty road. They wanted Jesus to know how happy they were that he was coming to their city.

More and more people were coming to greet Jesus. The people of Jerusalem were happy to welcome him. Everywhere Jesus looked, he saw smiling people and heard happy voices shout, **"Hosanna! Hosanna! Hosanna! Hosanna! Welcome is the one who comes in the name of the Lord!"**

Based on Luke 19:29-38.

Make Palm Branches

Supplies: scissors, different kinds of green crayons and markers (watercolor crayons, glitter crayons, color-changing crayons), tape or glue, tongue depressors or construction paper

Directions

• Copy the palm branch for each child. Cut out the palm branch for younger children. Give each child a palm branch. Write the child's name on the back of the branch.

• Let the children decorate the palm branch with different kinds of green crayons and markers (watercolor crayons, glitter crayons, color-changing crayons).

• Help each child make a handle for the palm branch. Give each child a tongue depressor. Help each child tape or glue the tongue depressor onto the branch.

• Or give each child a piece of construction paper. Show the children how to fold the paper in half, in half again, and in half again to make a narrow handle. The folds will make the handle more substantial. Help each child staple or tape the handle onto the back of the palm branch.

Have You Heard the News?

Arrange for a woman to pretend to be Mary and tell the story. The story should be told with feeling, animation, and excitement. Have a large scarf for the woman to drape over her head and shoulders. Ask the woman to excitedly rush into the room and interrupt, pretending to go to the tomb. The woman portraying Mary should breathlessly ask the children the questions and engage them into the story.

Before the woman comes in to tell the story, guide the children in pretending to go to the garden where the women discovered the empty tomb on Easter morning. Have the woman portraying Mary interrupt you at any time during this activity. When Mary comes in, help the children sit down to listen to her story.

Say: Let's pretend that we are Bible-times people and it is the first Easter morning. It is time to wake up. Let's walk to the garden. *(Walk in place.)* We see birds flying in the air. *(Flap arms like birds.)* We see flowers blooming. *(Cup hands.)* Let's smell the flowers. *(Sniff.)* We see a butterfly stretching its wings. *(Stretch out arms.)* When we see the beautiful garden, we remember our friend Jesus. We remember that Jesus is dead. He was buried in the garden tomb. We feel sad. *(Rub eyes as if crying.)* Wait a minute. What has happened? *(Stop suddenly.)* Look! *(Hold hands over eyes and look.)* Jesus is not here! He has risen! *(Clap hands with joy.)*

ave you heard the news? Have *you* heard the news? *(Repeat and ask a number of children individually.)* Did you know Jesus? Were you Jesus' friend? *(Ask each child a question.)* Well, come here. Gather around and sit down, and let me tell you the most amazing thing.

(The woman pretending to be Mary comes into the room. She tells the rest of the story.) My name is Mary. I'm a friend of Jesus. Today is Sunday. This morning another woman and I got up very early. We were going to the garden tomb. A tomb is a place where they bury people. Our best friend, Jesus, was dead. He was buried in the tomb. We were so sad. *(Look very sad.)* You won't believe it. I hardly can. The most amazing thing happened!

When we got to the tomb, Jesus was not there! That's right, the tomb was empty. We were so surprised! Then we noticed a young man sitting nearby. He said, *(Speak dramatically.)* "Jesus is not here. Jesus is alive."

Can you imagine how we felt? *(Pause.)* We did not understand it, but we were very happy! How would you have felt? *(Wait for responses.)* Well, we ran away from the tomb to go and find Jesus' other friends. We told them the good news. Jesus is alive!

I've got to go now and tell more people. Perhaps we'll meet again. Good-bye.

Based on Matthew 28:1-10.

Jesus Is Alive

by Daphna Flegal

Show the children how to rub their palms together to make a whishing sound. Let the children make the sound each time it appears in the story. Begin the story by talking in a whisper.

It was early in the morning. Everything was quiet in the garden. At one end of the garden was a tomb. A tomb is a place where they bury people.

Whish, whish. Whish, whish. (Rub palms together to make whishing sound.) It was so quiet, Mary Magdalene could hear her footsteps as she walked slowly across the grass to the tomb. She was very sad. Her friend, Jesus, was dead. He was buried in the tomb.

Whish, whish. (Louder. Rub palms together to make whishing sound.) Suddenly Mary Magdalene stopped. *(Stop rubbing hands.)* The huge rock in front of the tomb was gone! She looked into the tomb. It was empty!

"Jesus is not in the tomb," said Mary Magdalene. "I don't know where he is." She began to cry.

"Why are you crying?" asked a voice.

"I don't know where my friend Jesus is," answered Mary Magdalene.

"Mary," said the voice.

Mary Magdalene stopped crying and turned around. It was Jesus! Jesus was alive!

Whish, whish, whish. (Rub palms together to make whishing sound.) Mary Magdalene ran quickly out of the garden back to the city. She wanted to tell Jesus' friends the good news.

(Excitedly.) "Jesus is alive!" Mary Magdalene shouted with joy. "Jesus is alive!"

Based on John 20:1-18.

Early in the Morning

by Daphna Flegal

It was early in the morning,
The first day of the week.
(Hold up one finger.)

A woman came to the garden tomb,
So sad, she began to weep.
(Rub eyes as if weeping.)

"Woman, why are you weeping?"
Said two angels sitting there.
(Hold up two fingers.)

"They've taken away my Lord," she said.
"And I do not know where."
(Shake head no.)

The woman turned and saw a man
Standing in the morning light.
(Turn around.)

At first she didn't know who he was.
Then she cried out with delight.
(Cup hands around mouth.)

The man standing there was Jesus.
She could hardly believe her eyes.
(Point to eyes.)

The woman ran to tell her friends,
"Jesus was alive!"
(Raise arms up in praise.)

Based on John 20:11-18.

Easter Echoes

by Daphna Flegal

Have the children echo each phrase and motion after you, just the way you say and do them.

(Whisper.) Jesus is alive.
(Cup hands around mouth.)

(Normal voice.) Jesus is alive.
(Sign the word Jesus.)

(Excitedly!) Jesus is alive!
(Raise arms above head.)

Based on Matthew 28:5-7.

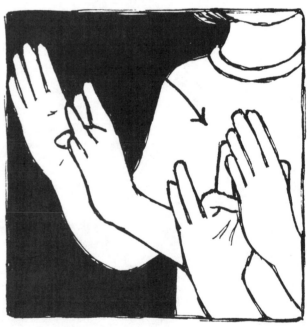

Five Little Children

by Daphna Flegal

Five little children
Came to church on Easter Day.
(Wiggle all five fingers.)
The first child said,
"Let's all shout hurray."
(Hold up one finger.)
The second child said,
"God brings new life in spring."
(Hold up two fingers.)
The third child said,
"Hear the church bells ring."
(Hold up three fingers.)
The fourth child said,
"Let's all sing for joy."
(Hold up four fingers.)
The fifth child said,
"God loves every girl and boy."
(Hold up five fingers.)
Five little children
Came to church to learn and play.
They all knew Easter was a very happy day.
(Wiggle all five fingers.)

Easter Day

by Joyce Riffe

Flowers are growing.
(Cup hands to make a flower.)
Green leaves are showing.
(Hold hands up, wiggle fingers.)
Baby robins spread their wings.
(Flap arms as if flying.)

I am so happy,
So very happy,
For the new life springtime brings.
(Hold arms out, turn around.)

Soft spring showers
*(Hold hands above head,
wiggle fingers and bring hands down.)*
Water new flowers.
(Cup hands to make a flower.)
Baby rabbits run and play.
*(Hold up first two fingers,
make hands hop.)*

God has planned
All new life around us
That we see on Easter Day.
(Hold arms out, turn around.)

Pentecost and the Early Church

Today Is Pentecost
by Daphna Flegal

Let the children sign "happy birthday" when it appears in the poem.

Today is Pentecost.
It's a very special day.
It's a time to wave red spirals.
It's a time to shout and say:
Happy birthday, church!

Today is Pentecost.
Let's celebrate today.
Let's listen to the wind.
Let's move our hands and say:
Happy birthday, church!

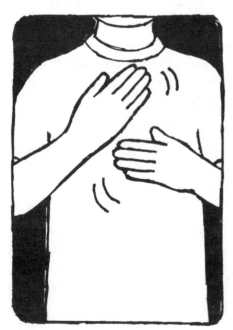

Happy

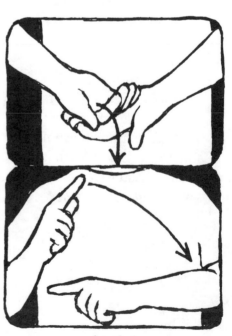

birthday

Whooosh! Whooosh!
by Susan Isbell

Give each child red crepe paper streamers or ribbons. Let the children wave their streamers each time you say, **"Who-o-o-sh! Who-o-o-sh!"** Or have the children pretend to be the wind by blowing, waving their arms in front of their bodies, and rocking side to side each time you say, **"Who-o-o-sh! Who-o-o-sh!"**

"**H**urry!" said Peter. "Come in quickly!"

James and John hurried into the room. They saw many of Jesus' friends already in the room. The friends were sitting together.

Who-o-o-sh! Who-o-o-sh! The sound of the wind rushed through the room. Peter heard the sound.

Who-o-o-sh! Who-o-o-sh! The sound of the wind rushed through the room. James and John heard the sound.

Who-o-o-sh! Who-o-o-sh! The sound of the wind rushed through the room. The friends heard the sound.

Who-o-o-sh! Who-o-o-sh! Peter was excited! He knew that God was with him.

Who-o-o-sh! Who-o-o-sh! James and John were excited. They knew that God was with them.

Who-o-o-sh! Who-o-o-sh! The friends were excited. They knew that God was with them.

The friends all started talking at once. They all wanted to tell everyone about Jesus. They wanted to tell everyone that God was with them.

Based on Acts 2:1-6, 28.

A Noisy Pentecost
by Daphna Flegal

Have the children repeat the words and sounds printed in italics.

Whisper. *Whisper. Whisper.* The friends of Jesus were talking quietly with each other. They were all together in one place for a special celebration called Pentecost.

Shh. Shh. Shh. Suddenly everyone stopped whispering. They heard a very loud noise.

Whoooo. Whoooo. Whoooo. The noise sounded like the wind blowing.

Sparkle. Sparkle. Sparkle. The friends of Jesus saw bright lights in the room. The lights looked like fire.

Chatter. Chatter. Chatter. Everyone started talking at once. Everyone was excited. They all knew that God was with them.

Mumble. Mumble. Mumble. The people in the city wondered what was happening.

"Listen. Listen. Listen." Peter said to the people. "We cannot keep from speaking about what we have seen and heard." Peter told the people all about Jesus.

Good news! Good news! Good news! Many people believed the good news about Jesus. Many people became followers of Jesus.

Happy birthday, church! The followers of Jesus became the very first church. Pentecost was the birthday of the church. *Happy birthday, church!*

Based on Acts 2:1, 4, 14, 32, 41.

Friends of Jesus

by Susan Isbell

Many friends of Jesus met together
every day.
(Hold up both hands, wiggle ten fingers.)
They shared with each other in many
special ways.
(Clasp hands together with fingers interlocking.)
Some friends shared by giving bread
and honey.
*(Hold up one hand, wiggle five fingers,
put other hand behind your back.)*
Other friends shared by giving
land and money.
*(Hold up the other hand, wiggle five fingers,
put the first hand behind your back.)*
Many friends of Jesus met together
every day.
(Hold up both hands, wiggle ten fingers.)
They shared with each other in many
special ways.
(Clasp hands together with fingers interlocking.)

Based on Acts 4:32-34.
© 1994 Cokesbury.

This Follower of Jesus

by Joyce Riffe

This follower of Jesus liked to
praise and pray.
(Hold up one finger on one hand.)
This follower of Jesus learned
more every day.
(Hold up two fingers on one hand.)
This follower of Jesus liked to meet and sing.
(Hold up three fingers on one hand.)
This follower of Jesus gave thanks
for everything.
(Hold up four fingers on one hand.)
This follower of Jesus met with friends to eat,
(Hold up five fingers on one hand.)
Loving,
(Hold up one finger on other hand.)
Sharing,
(Hold up two fingers on other hand.)
Helping,
(Hold up three fingers on other hand.)
Caring,
(Hold up four fingers on other hand.)
When they came to meet.
(Clasp hands together with fingers interlaced.)

Based on Acts 2:42-47.
© 1996 Cokesbury.

Followers of Jesus

by Joyce Riffe

Have the children sign the name Jesus each time it appears in the story.

The disciples told others the good news about **Jesus**. Many people were happy to hear the disciples tell about **Jesus**. Many people became followers of **Jesus**.

The followers of **Jesus** met together. They learned more and more about **Jesus**. They prayed together. They sang songs to praise God and thank God for **Jesus**. They met in each other's houses. They ate special meals together to remember **Jesus**. They took care of each other.

More and more people learned the good news about **Jesus**. More and more people became followers of **Jesus**. Everyone was happy to be together, to praise God, and to remember **Jesus**.

Based on Acts 2:41-42, 46-47.

Peter Heals a Man
by Patricia Ann Meyers

Peter and his friend John were going to the Temple to pray. *(Pretend to walk in place.)*

When they came near the gate, they saw a poor man who could not walk. *(Let the children crawl.)*

The man held out his hand for money and said, "I am a poor man who cannot walk. Will you give me some money, please?" *(Have the children hold out their hands.)*

Peter said, "I have no money, but we can help you walk." *(Shake head no; show empty hands with palms up.)*

Peter held out his hand to the man and said, "God loves you! Get up!" *(Children say, "God loves you; get up!" and help each other get up.)*

The man was so happy that he jumped up and down. He danced and clapped his hands. *(Children jump and clap.)*

The man thanked Peter and walked and danced all around to show others. He went to the Temple to thank God. *(Lead the children around the room walking and dancing with joy.)*

Based on Acts 3:1-10.

A New Name

by Susan Isbell

ractice the response **"We are called Christians"** with the children. Show the children the word *Christian* in American Sign Language. Each time you see the word in the story, make the sign for *Christian*. Have the children say the response, **"We are called Christians,"** each time you make the sign.

Barnabas traveled many places teaching and preaching about Jesus. The disciples were happy that Barnabas loved teaching others about Jesus, so they gave him a special job.

"Barnabas, the followers of Jesus in Antioch need someone to teach them more about Jesus," the disciples told him. "We want you to go and teach them."

Barnabas was glad to go. He knew that there was a lot of work to do in Antioch, so he took his friend Paul to Antioch with him.

The followers of Jesus who lived in Antioch had much to learn and much to tell.

"Because we follow Jesus the Christ, *(sign)* **we are called Christians,**" they told Barnabas and Saul.

"What a wonderful name!" Barnabas and Paul thought. "We are also followers of Jesus the Christ. That means that *(sign)* **we are called Christians,**" they said.

As long as they were in Antioch, they met more and more followers of Jesus. Each time they would meet, they would remind one another that *(sign)* **we are called Christians.**

When their work was done, Barnabas returned to the disciples in Jerusalem.

"Friends," he said, "in Antioch followers of Jesus are known by a new name. Because we follow Jesus the Christ, *(sign)* **we are called Christians.**"

Soon all the followers of Jesus the Christ were called by their new name. Everywhere they went, they would meet others who would say, *(sign)* **"We are called Christians."**

Note: Paul is used this story instead of the name Saul in order to lessen confusion for young children.

Based on Acts 11:19-26.

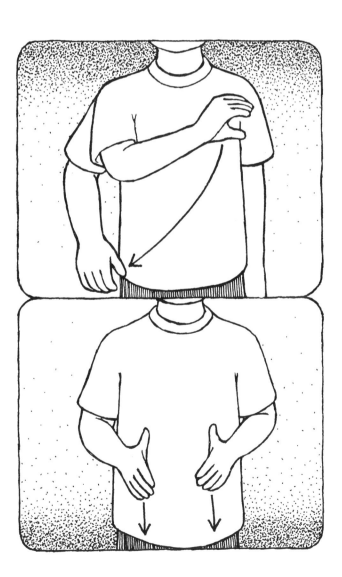

See the Secret Sign
by Daphna Flegal

Have the children make secret fish signs to use with the poem. Or pour a layer of sand into a shallow container or box lid. Have the children gather around the sand. Say the poem for the children. When you say, **"See the secret sign,"** use your finger to draw the outline of a fish (see below) in the sand. Repeat the poem enough times to give each child an opportunity to draw the fish in the sand.

Draw a fish in the sand.
  Shh, shh, shh.
  (Whisper, put finger to lips.)
Tell our friends across the land,
  See the secret sign.
  (Hold up fish signs.)

Welcome, followers of Jesus' way.
  Shh, shh, shh.
  (Whisper, put finger to lips.)
Come, meet here to sing and pray.
  See the secret sign.
  (Hold up fish signs.)

© 1996 Cokesbury.

Make Secret Fish Signs

Supplies: scissors, crayons or markers or fine sand, glue, glue brushes or cotton swabs, box lid or shallow tray

Directions

• Copy the secret fish sign for each child. Cut out the fish for younger children. Write the child's name on the back of the sign.

• Let the children decorate the fish sign with crayons or markers.

• Or let the children decorate the fish sign with sand. Have the children use glue brushes or cotton swabs to brush glue on their fish signs. Set each sign in a box lid or shallow tray. Show each child how to sprinkle fine sand over the sign. Shake off the excess glue into a trash container.

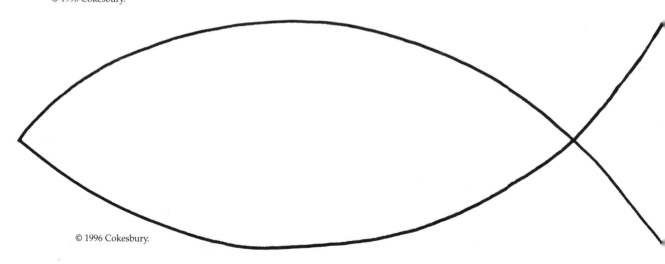

© 1996 Cokesbury.

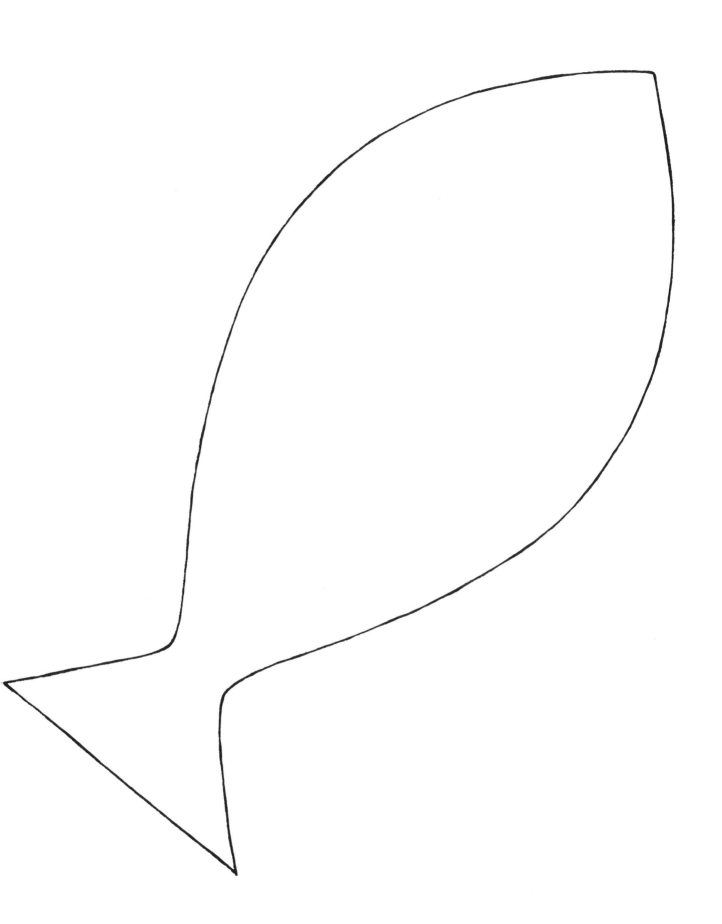

Paul Makes a Change

by Daphna Flegal

Use the Paul mad/glad puppets (see directions at right) to tell this story. Have the children hold up their puppets to the mad side when they hear the word **mad.** Have the children turn their puppets to the glad side each time they hear the word **glad.**

Paul was **mad.**

"I don't like the followers of Jesus," said Paul. "I don't believe what they say about Jesus."

Paul was **mad.**

"I'm going to another city," said Paul. "I will find the followers of Jesus and put them in jail."

Paul was **mad.** He gathered some men to go with him and started out down the road.

Suddenly a bright light shone all around Paul. Paul fell to the ground.

"Paul, Paul," said a voice. "Why are you being unkind to my friends?"

"Who are you?" asked Paul.

"I am Jesus," said the voice. "Get up and go to the city. I will teach you what to do."

Paul got up. He still could not see, so the men led him to the city. Paul did not understand what had happened, but he knew he had changed. Paul was no longer **mad.**

Paul was **glad.** Jesus showed him how to love others.

Paul was **glad.** He believed Jesus.

Paul was **glad.** He became a follower of Jesus.

Based on Acts 9:1-9.

Make Paul Mad/Glad Puppets

Supplies: scissors, crayons, glue or tape, craft sticks

Directions

• Copy the Paul mad/glad puppet faces for each child. Cut out the faces for younger children. Give each child a mad face.

• **Say: Paul did not like people who followed Jesus. He was mad that Jesus' friends were telling others about Jesus.**

• Give each child a glad face.

• **Say: Something happened to make Paul glad. God helped Paul learn to be a follower of Jesus.**

• Let the children decorate the faces with crayons.

• Help the children glue or tape the faces back to back onto craft sticks. Show the children how to turn their puppets to show the mad faces and then the glad faces.

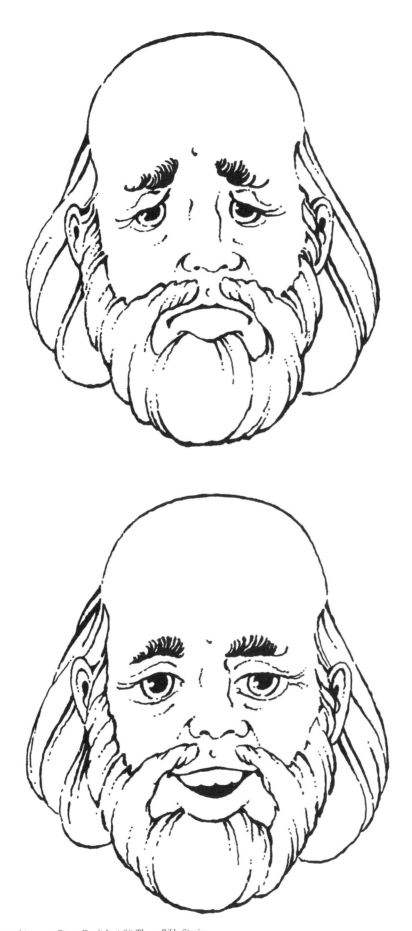

Paul and Barnabas

by Daphna Flegal

Use the Paul glad puppet (page 101) and the blank face (below) to make turnaround puppets to use with this poem.

Paul and Barnabas traveled
(Hold up the Paul side of the puppets.)
To places far away.
They told others about Jesus.
And living in God's way.

I can be a missionary,
(Turn to the child side of the puppets.)
Like Barnabas and like Paul.
I can share the love of God
To people big and small.

Based on Acts 15:35.
© 1991 Graded Press.

Make Turnaround Puppets
Supplies: scissors, crayons, glue or tape

Directions
• Copy the Paul glad puppet face and the blank face for each child. Cut out the faces for younger children.

• Give each child the Paul puppet face. Let the children decorate the faces with crayons.

• Give each child the blank face. Let the children decorate the face to be their own faces.

• Help the children glue or tape their faces back to back onto craft sticks.

• Show the children how to turn their puppets to show the Paul faces and then their own faces.

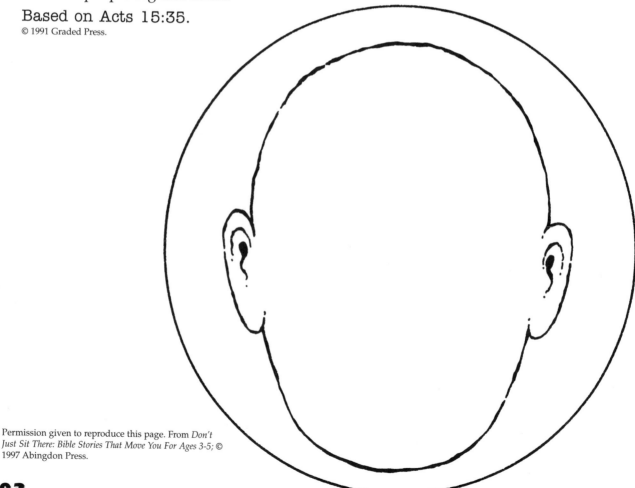

Lydia, Lydia
by Daphna Flegal

Make Lydia dolls (see below) to use with the poem. Have the children hold up their Lydia puppets each time they hear, **"Lydia, Lydia."**

Lydia, Lydia,
Dressed in purple,
What are you doing today?
I'm sitting here beside the river,
To talk with friends and pray.

Lydia, Lydia,
Dressed in purple,
What are you doing today?
I'm sitting here beside the river,
Hearing what Paul has to say.

Lydia, Lydia,
Dressed in purple,
What are you doing today?
I'm sitting here beside the river.
I heard about Jesus today.

Based on Acts 16:11-15.

Make Lydia Dolls
Supplies: roundhead clothespins, crayon or marker, scrap of purple cloth or crepe paper, glue

Directions
• Give each child a roundhead clothespin. Let the children use a crayon or marker to draw a face on the clothespin.
• Help each child glue a scrap of purple cloth or purple crepe paper around the clothespin to make a Bible-times robe for the Lydia dolls.

Priscilla and Aquila
by Daphna Flegal

Have the children repeat **"Priscilla and Aquila"** at the end of each stanza.

Paul had two friends,
(Hold up two fingers.)
Can you say their names?
Priscilla and Aquila.

They worked together
To make their tents.
(Hold tips of fingers together to make a tent.)
Priscilla and Aquila.

They worked together
To tell about Jesus.
(Cup hands around mouth.)
Priscilla and Aquila.

Paul had two friends,
Can you say their names?
(Hold up two fingers.)
Priscilla and Aquila.

Based on Acts 18:1-4.

Good News! Good News! Hear Us Yell

by Daphna Flegal

Have the children repeat, **"Good news! Good news! Hear us yell,"** and do the motions.

Paul and his friends
Had good news to tell.
Good news! Good news! Hear us yell.
(Cup hands around mouth.)

Ananias helped Paul see again.
He and Paul became good friends.
Paul and his friends
Had good news to tell.
Good news! Good news! Hear us yell.
(Cup hands around mouth.)

Barnabas said, "Paul, come with me."
They took money to people in need.
Paul and his friends
Had good news to tell.
Good news! Good news! Hear us yell.
(Cup hands around mouth.)

Priscilla and Aquila worked with Paul.
They made tents both big and small.
Paul and his friends
Had good news to tell.
Good news! Good news! Hear us yell.
(Cup hands around mouth.)

Lydia met Paul by the river one day.
She became a follower of Jesus' way.

Paul and his friends
Had good news to tell.
Good news! Good news! Hear us yell.
(Cup hands around mouth.)

Timothy met Paul as a young man.
He gave Paul a helping hand.
Paul and his friends
Had good news to tell.
Good news! Good news! Hear us yell.
(Cup hands around mouth.)

Based on Acts 9:1-22, 26-28; 16:1-2, 4, 11-15; 18:1-3.

Sunday School, The Bible, and Other Things

This Is My Church
by Sue Downing

This is my church.
(Place fingertips together to make steeple.)
The doors open wide.
(Move arms out.)
See all the people praying inside.
(Bow head and fold hands.)

Here in my church
(Place fingertips together to make a steeple.)
I sing and I pray.
(Bow head and fold hands.)
My teacher reads stories.
(Hold hands as if reading a book.)
I work and I play.
(Act out coloring or building with blocks.)

Here in my church
(Place fingertips together to make a steeple.)
I'm happy as can be,
(Smile a big smile.)
For I'm one of the people
(Point to self.)
In God's church, you see!
(Place fingertips together to make a steeple.)

Colored Windows

My church has colored windows,
(Touch fingertips together to make a steeple.)
Red, yellow, green, and blue.
(Hold up first, second, third, and fourth fingers.)
Let's look out the windows,
(Spread fingers apart, look through fingers.)
See the colors shining through.
(Wiggle fingers.)

The world becomes a rainbow,
(Make an arch with hands.)
Red, yellow, green, and blue.
(Hold up first, second, third, and fourth fingers.)
When we look out the windows,
(Spread fingers apart, look through fingers.)
And see the colors shining through.
(Wiggle fingers.)

The Bible
by Ellen Shepard

The Bible is a special book,
(Hold hands like an open Bible.)
God's words are written there;
(Point at one open hand.)
And when I turn each page to look,
(Pretend to turn pages.)
I handle it with care.
(Nod head.)

Learning to Be Kind

Five happy children standing in a line.
(Hold up five fingers.)
The first child said,
"God wants us to be kind."
(Hold up one finger.)
The second child said,
"I'll bring food for those in need."
(Hold up two fingers.)
The third child said,
"I'll bring storybooks to read."
(Hold up three fingers.)
The fourth child said,
I'll bring pennies I can share."
(Hold up four fingers.)
The fifth child said,
"There are many ways to care."
(Hold up five fingers.)
Five happy children standing in a line.
All were happy sharing
and learning to be kind.
(Wiggle all five fingers.)

That's What Jesus Said to Do
by Elizabeth Crocker

I stretch my fingers way up high.
*(Reach up to ceiling with fingertips
as far as you can reach.)*

I reach from side to side.
(Extend arms side to side.)

I'll give myself a great big hug.
*(Wrap arms across your chest
with a hugging motion.)*

There's so much love inside.
(Continue hugging. Sway from side to side.)

The God who made me put it there.
(Point to heart.)

God put it there for me to share.
*(Point to heart, then extend hands forward,
palms up.)*

I'll give my love to God and you.
(Trace a big heart in the air.)

That's what Jesus said to do.
(Nod head as if saying yes.)

God Is Always With Us

Have the children make a fist and move their
arms towards their bodies as they shout **"Yes!"**

Is God with you when
you're fast asleep?
Yes!
Is God with you when you brush your teeth?
Yes!
Is God with you when you're feeling sad?
Yes!
Is God with you when you're feeling glad?
Yes!
Is God with you when you're watching TV?
Yes!
Is God with you when you're playing
with me?
Yes!
Is God with you when you talk
on the phone?
Yes!
Is God with you when you're helping
at home?
Yes!
Is God with you when you're singing a song?
Yes!
Is God with you all the day long?
Yes!

God Is Love

by Daphna Flegal

Have the children use their two index fingers
to draw a heart in the air each time they hear
you repeat the Bible verse in the poem.

It doesn't matter who you are,
Or where your family lives.
God loves everyone, everywhere.
That's just the way God is.
God is love.

God loves the baby, oh, so small.
God loves the mother too.
God loves the young man grown so tall.
God loves me and you.

It doesn't matter who you are,
Or where your family lives.
God loves everyone, everywhere,
That's just the way God is.
God is love.

God loves the girl with braids in her hair.
God loves her grandpa too.
God loves the boy in his motorized chair.
God loves me and you.

It doesn't matter who you are,
Or where your family lives.
God loves everyone, everywhere,
That's just the way God is.
God is love.

God loves the woman who speaks with
her hands.
God loves her brother too.
God loves all people in every land.
God loves me and you.

It doesn't matter who you are,
Or where your family lives.
God loves everyone, everywhere,
That's just the way God is.
God is love.

Jesus and Me

by Sue Downing

With my eyes I can see
(Point to eyes.)
Ways to help you and me.

With my mouth I can tell
(Point to mouth.)
Stories of Jesus that I know so well!

With my hands
(Hold out hands.)
There's a lot to do.
I can hug,
(Hug oneself.)
give help,
(Outstretch arms.)
and paint a picture for you.
(Pretend to paint.)

With my feet I can go here and there,
(Move legs up and down.)
Spreading God's love everywhere.
(Cross arms over heart.)

With my ears, shoulders,
elbows, and knees,
(Point to body parts.)
I can serve Jesus with all of these!
(Lift arms up.)

ndex of Bible References

ndex of Titles